TAKING CHANCES, MAKING CHOICES

TAKING CHANCES, MAKING CHOICES

ONE WOMAN'S WILLINGNESS
TO TAKE DARING CHANCES,
MAKE BOLD CHOICES,
AND FOLLOW HER DREAMS.

KATHERYNE STONE

Copyright © 2022 by Katheryne Stone.

All rights reserved. No part of this book may be used or reproduced in any manner whatsoever without prior written consent of the author, except as provided by the United States of America copyright law.

Published by Advantage, Charleston, South Carolina.
Member of Advantage Media.

ADVANTAGE is a registered trademark, and the Advantage colophon is a trademark of Advantage Media Group, Inc.

Printed in the United States of America.

10 9 8 7 6 5 4 3 2 1

ISBN: 978-1-64225-552-2 (Paperback)
ISBN: 978-1-64225-551-5 (eBook)

LCCN: 2022917070

Cover design by Matthew Morse.
Layout design by Amanda Haskin.

This publication is designed to provide accurate and authoritative information in regard to the subject matter covered. It is sold with the understanding that the publisher is not engaged in rendering legal, accounting, or other professional services. If legal advice or other expert assistance is required, the services of a competent professional person should be sought.

> Advantage Media helps busy entrepreneurs, CEOs, and leaders write and publish a book to grow their business and become the authority in their field. Advantage authors comprise an exclusive community of industry professionals, idea-makers, and thought leaders. Do you have a book idea or manuscript for consideration? We would love to hear from you at **AdvantageMedia.com**.

Now to Him who is able to do exceeding abundantly beyond all that we ask or think, according to the power that works within us, to Him be the glory in the church and in Christ Jesus to all generations forever and ever.

—*Ephesians 3:20–21*

TO MY GRANDCHILDREN: HARRISON, PEYTON, BAILEY, TURNER, AUDREY, OLIVIA, AND CHARLOTTE.

AND TO THEIR GRANDCHILDREN—
AND ALL WHO COME AFTER.

REMEMBER TO PASS ON THE LEGACY
AND THE STORIES!

CONTENTS

ACKNOWLEDGMENTS 1

INTRODUCTION. 3

PART I 7
RAISING A FAMILY AND BUILDING A BUSINESS

CHAPTER 1 9
CHOICES AND CONSEQUENCES

CHAPTER 2 19
TAKE TWO

CHAPTER 3 27
TWO SKIPPERS, ONE SHIP

CHAPTER 4 35
I MARRIED A RISK TAKER

PART II 47
LESSONS ALONG THE WAY

CHAPTER 5 49
LEARNING TO LAUGH

CHAPTER 6 55
LEARNING TO LEAD

CHAPTER 7 63
MONEY AND MATTERS OF THE HEART

PART III 73
A LIVING LEGACY

CHAPTER 8 75
FAMILY IS EVERYTHING

CHAPTER 9 85
GENERATIONS OF GENEROSITY

CHAPTER 10 93
THE POWER OF ONE

PART IV 103
COLLECTED ESSAYS

CONCLUSION 115

ABOUT THE AUTHOR 117

ACKNOWLEDGMENTS

My sincere thanks to everyone at Advantage Media who helped make this book possible—especially to Beth, who not only heard my voice but listened to my heart. Your unending questions made me think and remember, and your encouragement and "chats" kept me returning to the project when I thought it was too hard.

Many people have passed through my life, and I'm so very grateful for every one of you—for your influence, the lessons, and the fun. Many are a part of this written view of my life, and I appreciate you allowing me to share your stories along with mine. Your friendships mean more to me than you may realize.

Lastly, thanks to my husband, my sons and their wives, and my grandchildren (and that precious new great-grandson!) for sticking with me, listening to my stories, and helping make this dream to write a book become a reality. A very special hug to the one whose idea it was!

INTRODUCTION

I get my love of storytelling from my grandmother, Mom Brown. As a young girl, I often spent the night with her at the ranch. On the long drives there, she would tell stories of her life. One of my favorites was about her finally letting a boy drive her home from church one evening in her daddy's buckboard. After a bit, he managed to get his arm on the back of the seat, then onto her shoulder. She hollered, "Whoa!" The old mule stopped immediately. Nothing the boy said got that old mule moving again, so he got off the buckboard to try. As soon as he stepped out, Mom Brown hollered, "Go on!" Off the mule trotted, leaving that fresh young man in the dark, alone, and with a healthy walk home. I'd always ask what happened to him, and Mom Brown would always say that he was probably still trying to get home. She laughed every time she told that story.

When I reflect on why I always loved my grandmother's stories so much, I believe it was because it brought me closer to her, to who she was, and to who I was. It's humbling when you make the connection that every member of your family, even back to those you have never met, has influenced you and has on some level contributed to the person you are today. A strong motivation for writing this book—for *telling my stories*—was to let my grandchildren and great-grandchildren really know who their grandparents are. To share with them our legacy of family, friends, colleagues, franchisees, and mentors who touched our lives, taught us life lessons (both good and bad), and inspired us along the way.

As I began to gather my stories, I realized that a big part of my life has been teaching and mentoring. I taught a professional workshop for several years called *Think*, and my primary goal for that workshop was to get people to think differently and to think bigger. For Kent and me, changing our thinking made all the difference in our professional life, and those positive differences flowed into our personal life. In the early days of starting a business, we were happy to settle for whatever came. We had a wide variety of experiences in those early days, but we didn't consciously consider what lessons we might draw from them. We just kept plowing through. Yes, we worked hard, and we did the right things, but it was through our willingness to listen to and learn from our own mentors and teachers that we began to realize our full potential.

My own professional and personal growth inspired me to formulate ways to help other people think differently. To help people think about how they were going about their life, how they were being influenced and how they were influencing others, and whether they were taking time to learn from their experiences. I hope reading my stories prompts you to think a little bit differently, to say, "I've never thought about it like that before," or to realize that you can make your subconscious work for you or that goal setting is important, or—my personal favorite—your *why*. Why do you work? And no, the answer is not, "The money."

Finally, I hope my stories help you find a way to give back. Whether it's time or money or teaching or mentoring or whatever your unique gift is, I hope you pay it forward.

PART I

RAISING A FAMILY AND BUILDING A BUSINESS

We have all wondered and worried about our "double lives." I mean our lives of working at home and working outside too. Family has always been most important to Kent and me. As we started out, working sometimes seemed to be taking over that "most important" position.

Whether you are an employee, an employer, or are self-employed, working while building a home and raising a family is quite a challenge. Maybe you will identify with some of my stories.

CHAPTER 1

CHOICES AND CONSEQUENCES

As a young woman, I always felt comfortable in my own skin and in the satisfaction that I was doing things "right." I followed the rules and would never dare cause a scene—but I was also fiercely independent and never afraid to speak my mind. At twenty-five, I landed my first professional job as an executive assistant at the largest investment counseling firm in the Southwest. I was an excellent employee—hard-working, dependable—and I knew how to do things right. My job description included dictation, scheduling appointments, making travel arrangements, typing reports, and performing other usual office duties. My boss was smart, high powered … and completely disorganized. Much of my time was spent redoing things. He would start down one path, then switch gears and go another. It was extremely time consuming and frustrating for me. One day I decided, in my infinite wisdom, to help move things along. I told him it would be extremely helpful if he would take some time to gather his thoughts before we spent several hours working together.

Usually very loud and verbal, he looked at me and quietly said, "Mrs. Stone, I hired you to make my life and my job easier. Anytime you can't or don't want to do that, I'll give you an excellent reference." He went on to explain that if he were organized, anyone could help him. He needed someone who knew how to manage his disorganization so he could get on with his own job. He needed someone who could take chaos and turn out great results. He thought that was me.

It was a slap in the face. I took pride in doing things right, and it never occurred to me that others didn't see it the same way. Mr. Green's response was a revelation to me that I had the right to *choose* my job, *and* he had the *right* to tell me how to do it. It was an important lesson about choices and the rights and responsibilities that are a consequence of those choices. My work, my job wasn't about me. It was about serving my boss. Not because I had to but because I chose to do so. The reason I chose to work for him under difficult circumstances wasn't because the job was always fun or easy. It was because there were other things in my life that were important to me. Building a home, taking care of my family, improving our lifestyle. Work is what you do so that you can do the other things you want to do in life.

It was now clear to me that if I chose to work there, it was my responsibility to do whatever it took to make his job easier. That is why he hired me. If it meant doing it over, and if it meant living with his disorganization, it was his right to expect me to do just that. Now I had a choice to make—and I chose to quit. I told Mr. Green that I decided I wanted to stay home to be with my children.

The truth was that my pride and the pressures of the job had gotten the best of me. But I needed that job and the salary and perks it provided. My husband and I had just moved our growing family to a larger home in Houston, and with that came a bigger mortgage. In fact, that bigger mortgage was the reason I'd gone back to work. It was a great opportunity for improvement, the salary was amazing, and the benefits were extraordinary in anybody's book. Now, I had gone and quit.

Fortunately, within a month Mr. Green called and asked me to come back, telling me that he knew we could work things out. I returned with a new appreciation for the opportunity this job provided and was committed to making it work, but now I also knew it was always my choice to stay. I did quit again a few years later—but not before I was almost fired.

It was during my employee evaluation at the end of my first year, not long after Mr. Green had asked me to return, when he said, "There's a mistake in your file."

"What do you mean?" I asked.

"It doesn't show your degree."

"Mr. Green, I don't have a degree."

He said, "What college did you graduate from?"

"I didn't graduate from college."

"That's impossible," he said. "You have to have a degree to work here."

I didn't realize at the time that everyone at the company—even the mail clerks—had college degrees. I'm not sure how it was missed in my interview process, but there it was: college degrees were required, and I didn't have one. The human resources supervisor told me that unfortunately I could no longer work there. Luckily for me, Mr. Green intervened. He called me into his office and said, "This is not something you are to talk about to anybody else in the company, but you're not leaving."

While the experience made me more conscious of my environment and how I fit in (or didn't), it also gave me power. I now knew that I could survive the fear of losing my job and that I could survive being told that I'm not as smart as I thought I was. This new perspective also made me think of my childhood differently. I was raised in the country, in a very conservative small town in South Texas. My mother was very proper. We always had to say the right thing, do the right thing, look the right way—and what was "right" was based on a very narrow perspective. I was raised to believe that doing the right thing the right way all the time to the best of my ability would be enough. But now I realized that wasn't enough. It was important to ask questions, learn new skills, and always try to improve and grow.

> **I now knew that I could survive the fear of losing my job and that I could survive being told that I'm not as smart as I thought I was.**

The office was filled with educated, wealthy people. The man who owned the company had an art collection displayed at the office. I went to work one day to find a beautiful new painting in my office. He asked if I liked it. "Well, it's very different," I said. It was an abstract by Rothko costing hundreds of thousands of dollars. I had no knowledge of fine art at the time. Today that painting is priceless. Learning to fit into this environment without letting myself be intimidated was a good lesson. It also taught me that I needed to keep stretching myself to learn more and that if I didn't want to do that, I had the choice to leave and go work somewhere else. I could find a job where I was the most educated person in the office if I wanted to—but I knew that wasn't what I wanted.

What I wanted was the best job with the best benefits and the best salary, because my goal was to improve our home life. If I was going to work, to leave my kids, and deal with that double life of being both a mom and a career woman, I wanted to have the best job available to me. I wasn't necessarily seeking out a lifetime career, but I was not going to waste my time making minimum wage in a stagnant job where I couldn't grow and learn.

Over the next few years, I continued to expand my skills and abilities at work and do my best to keep up with the demands of the job while juggling my roles as wife and mother. Those were challenging years. Kent was working in retail at the time and not loving it. We had moved to Houston for a better job opportunity for him. We both had a three-hour commute round trip every day—let me tell you, that was tough. Any working parent knows the challenges of picking your child up at day care on time when you're stuck in traffic and the clock is ticking. I remember quite well one particular time when we pulled into the day care parking lot at 6:29 p.m.—and the day care closed at 6:30 p.m. We would soon find out that arriving in the nick of time was the least of our problems. Our oldest son was eight at the time, and our youngest was six.

That particular evening, Ray came out and got in the car first. "Where's your brother?" I asked.

"I don't know," he said.

"Well, go in and get him," I said.

Ray came back and told me his brother wasn't there. Now it was my turn to go in. Bryan was nowhere to be found, and the staff had no idea he was missing. I was hysterical. "What do you mean he's not here? What do you mean you don't know where my son is?"

We jumped in the car and raced home, hoping that's where Bryan went from school. It was the longest fifteen-minute ride of my life, and as we rounded the corner of our street, I saw my six-year-old son on the roof of our house with one leg in the chimney. I yelled for Kent to stop the car, and I ran toward our house screaming, "Bryan, get down from there!" Kids started piling out from the windows and doors of my house. My six-year-old son had walked home after school instead of going to day care and decided he would entertain the neighborhood children by demonstrating how Santa Claus comes down the chimney! The neighborhood gang had all been waiting at the fireplace for Bryan to make his entrance. We had gotten there just in time, and thankfully Bryan was safe, but it was a terrifying and crazy experience—and there would be more.

Little League practices and games came and went as we did our best to pay the bills, provide for our children, and capture as much time with them as we could. I'm not complaining. As with most things in life, we made a choice. We chose where we lived, we chose for me to work, and we chose where we worked. That's what was right for us. Today, that's still a conversation: whether moms should work outside the home or not and the guilt and consequences that go with either choice. As a working mom, you feel guilty, and you feel stressed all the time. It's always about other people at work and about your kids and husband at home—there's no time for yourself.

On the other side of the coin, I hear young mothers who stay at home today say they feel like their kids are underfoot all the time; they have such limited opportunities to be around other adults or time to do anything for themselves, and money is tight. I don't believe there is a right or wrong answer to this dilemma. I believe parents have to make the right choice for their family and understand and accept the consequences of that choice.

There were times when the boys were very young that I did choose to stay home, and I was grateful for that time, but I always knew that I wanted to work outside the home, and that had its own challenges. I felt like I was always looking for a better way to keep things (and myself) calm and collected. Time management at work is not nearly as challenging as time management at home! Mornings were especially stressful. Getting the boys up, dressed, fed, homework collected, school projects organized, lunch boxes prepared … you know the drill. I wasn't always calm and not always the sweet mama I wanted to be.

Bryan was creative and easily distracted and as a result was almost always late. One evening, Kent went in to say good night to find Bryan with his covers up to his ears. It was too warm for that, so Kent suggested he pull the covers down. "No!" shrieked Bryan, holding tightly to the blanket. Suspecting something awry, Kent pulled the covers down to discover our son was completely dressed for school—shoes and all.

"Why on earth are you dressed for school?" asked Kent. In a somewhat tearful voice, that sweet little boy said he didn't want to make us late in the morning, so he thought sleeping in his clothes was the solution. A humbling mama moment for me. I needed to do better, and I learned to organize more things at night to make mornings less stressful for *all* of us.

The constant motion that was our life didn't slow, but we acclimated to the choices we made and did our best to make it work. The boys were healthy and happy. I was managing the pressures of my job while learning everything I could, not only about the work itself but about art and travel and people. We were paying our bills, but while Kent was successful at his job, he no longer found it fulfilling and began looking to either change fields or get a promotion with the company he was working for. The promotion would have required us to move to Louisiana, and we didn't want to do that. Neither of us had thought of going into business for ourselves, but when the opportunity presented itself, Kent took it. The store he worked at needed someone to clean their carpets, and Kent asked me if I knew anyone who did that. I did—he was a SWAT officer who had a carpet-cleaning business on the side, so I set up his company to clean the carpets at the store. While there, he explained the business to Kent. It took him about two hours to complete the job, for which he charged $700. At the time, Kent was barely making that a month.

After getting all the details, Kent came home and asked me what I thought about us getting into the carpet-cleaning business for ourselves. I was horrified. I said, "I know you're unhappy, and I want you to get a job you want, but going into business for ourselves? We know nothing about that. How would we even do that? How would we come up with the money? How would we start?" We certainly didn't have extra money lying around to invest in carpet cleaning. I saw it as too great of a risk—I liked the security of my weekly paycheck. After many late-night conversations, a few tears, and pointless arguments, I decided to keep the security of my job and wished Kent luck with his new carpet-cleaning business. It was another choice, but a reluctant one.

As you will see later, it was a wise choice, but one that came with both good and hard consequences. Choose wisely, and be prepared for all consequences.

In just six months, Kent had begun to build an income-generating business, and one evening, after a very stressful day at work, I came home in tears. Kent said, "Look, you are very good at what you do, but do it for us instead of for another company. Quit your job." I thought about it for a couple of days, and then I turned in my resignation (for the last time) to Mr. Green. Although it had been a challenging job, I had come to appreciate all its life lessons and my newfound interests, which included a love of collecting art. It wasn't just the paycheck I would miss, but I knew it was the right decision for Kent, the boys, and me.

The adjustment to working for ourselves didn't come easily to me. Knowing neither one of us would be getting a guaranteed paycheck scared me to death. I am not a risk taker—I like security. I like to know that we have the money to cover the mortgage that is still due on the fifteenth along with all the other bills that would continue to come whether or not we had income to pay them.

As new business owners, we were shocked at how many customers didn't pay their bills, and we had to figure out how to collect the money due us. When it would get hard and customers wouldn't pay, I would panic. I can't count the number of times in those first years that I said to Kent, "You know what? I could go to work tomorrow, and in two weeks I'd have a paycheck and I'd know exactly the amount it would be." In those moments, Kent always asked me to give him two weeks, and he would go see the overdue customers and get the income we needed. It was Kent's unwavering belief in us that got us through those early years.

While our business didn't offer the security I craved, I did find benefits to working for ourselves, especially in the early days when I worked from home. For starters, I was home when my kids got home from school. I appreciated having that time with them, and I did not miss the stress of rushing all of us out the door in the mornings or rushing to pick them up at day care after work. I realized I could work in my pajamas if I wanted to—not that I ever did, but just knowing I could gave me a sense of freedom. One day, I did treat myself.

Kent called that afternoon and said, "Where are you?"

"I bought very long phone lines and ran them out the office window, and now I am sitting on the back patio in my swimsuit answering our business line."

Kent laughed and said, "So, you finally bought into being self-employed."

Six months later, the four of us were living in a hotel in Richardson.

THINGS TO CONSIDER

- Work is what you do so you can do other things you want to do in life.

- Make wise choices, and be prepared for any circumstance.

- Take chances for a better future.

- You can survive your kids' antics!

- Be organized, and you will be able to do more in less time.

CHAPTER 2

TAKE TWO

It was the spring of 1978, and we'd been in Houston for several years and in business for just a little over a year when the man who helped us get into the business in the first place called. "Why don't y'all sell your business in Houston, move to Richardson, and start a business here?"

And we did. It didn't seem like such a big deal at the time. I don't remember having much discussion about it. We just said, "Okay," sold our business, moved to Richardson, Texas, and started over. I look back now and wonder, *What was I thinking?*

Starting over, no matter how young and willing you are, is not without its challenges. There were a couple of months left until the end of the school year, so Kent moved to find us a place to live and start the business while the boys and I stayed in Houston until school was out.

Once school let out, the boys and I packed our belongings in a U-Haul and headed north. I was tired and nervous and excited to see our new home and get settled. It wasn't until we arrived that I found out we didn't have a home to go to. This was before cell phones or even personal computers, so Kent and I weren't able to constantly communicate with each other. As a result, one or the other of us was sometimes left in the dark, and boy was it dark.

> **Starting over, no matter how young and willing you are, is not without its challenges.**

The prospect of buying a house anytime soon was slim to none. Banks don't jump at the chance to finance someone who is self-employed and only had a business for a year before selling it and moving. It didn't help that the cash we had from selling the business in Houston had been put into the new business, leaving us cash poor. We needed to find another place to stay—and fast.

We knew we wanted to be close to where our new business was, and we found a motel that had a kitchenette. It was clean, comfortable enough, and convenient. The trailer filled with everything we owned was on the side of the road next to the motel. It wasn't a bad place, but after the first couple of nights I noticed there were a lot of comings and goings in the motel overnight. I told Kent it was best to keep the boys in the room and not let them venture outside.

"Why?" Kent asked.

"Because I think this is more than just a motel," I replied. We were horrified at the idea of our two young boys *living* in a motel with a pay-by-the-hour option and immediately looked for a new place to stay. We moved to another motel, which was much nicer and had a more stable clientele. We were there a couple of months while still desperately trying to buy a house. When I think back, I still can't believe how we managed it all from a motel. The boys started school, which meant homework and afternoon activities. In the mornings, we'd be busy with the business while the boys were at school—Kent shampooing carpets and looking for more customers, and me trying to keep the business's paper trail straight and the bills paid. In the afternoons and evenings, we put all our focus on the boys. Once they went to bed, we got right back to working on the business. We would take an extension cord out by the pool and plug in my electric typewriter, and I would type estimates in the dimming light of dusk. Somehow this new work-by-the-pool experience wasn't quite the same as the one I'd enjoyed in Houston. What had we gotten ourselves into?

Motel living grew more stressful and expensive. We couldn't continue to keep eating out all the time, so we tried to make do in our cramped quarters. I remember making tacos on a Coleman stove in the bathroom at one point! Now I can laugh at the ridiculousness of it all, but at the time it was hard to see the light at the end of the tunnel that would make it all worth it. We desperately continued our search for a house that we could afford and that we could finance. That desperate search led us to a Realtor who would become—and still is—one of the dearest people in my heart.

When we met Roxanne, we poured our hearts out to her. "Don't worry about it; my partner and I will find you a house," she said. I think it's moments like this when the Lord is thinking, *These people are going to need help*, and so He sent Roxanne.

As promised, Roxanne did find us a house. But she did so much more than that. The mortgage company wanted us to show we had extra money in a savings account that did not exist. Roxanne and her partner put $10,000 in a savings account in our name, not even putting their names on it. She just came to me and said, "Kathy, your closing is next week."

I asked, "How on earth have you worked that out?"

"Well," she said, "you have some money in a savings account."

"No, we don't," I said.

"Yes, you do. It will be there in your financials, and you can pay it back when you can."

Looking back over your life, you begin to see all the times that people just seem to show up when you need them most. Because of Roxanne, we were able to get our house. As soon as the house closed, we returned their $10,000. Years later, I asked Roxanne, "How many people have you done things like that for in your life?"

She just laughed and said, "Well, you weren't the first, and you weren't the only one, but it doesn't matter how many."

> **Looking back over your life, you begin to see all the times that people just seem to show up when you need them most.**

We settled into our new home and focused on getting the boys into a routine and growing the business. We got busy buying equipment, hiring people, and putting all our money back into our company. Things were moving right along, but we needed an influx of cash to push it to the next level. So, in less than two years of home ownership, we sold the house and invested the proceeds in the business. We rented for about a year, and oh, what a year it was!

Ray and Bryan were twelve and fourteen, we were renting again, and the business was beginning to flourish. We had no doubt that we would be homeowners once again in the near future. We were back on track, and then …

I realized I was pregnant.

As it was my third pregnancy, I knew instantly, and I wasn't happy about it. I didn't handle it well at all. I didn't even tell Kent for a couple of months. I was almost thirty-seven, I had two boys, and I didn't want three. I struggled coming to terms with it. In fact, when

Kent tells the story, he says he thought I was either going to divorce him or have a nervous breakdown, because I was so mad all the time.

I called my mother a couple of times to tell her, but I was so upset, I couldn't even say it. I would just cry. I didn't tell anyone, and I didn't go to the doctor, because I just knew.

When I was two months along, we went to Houston for a company meeting that my mother would also be attending. I made an appointment to see the doctor while we were there, and as I'd finally told my mother, she insisted on going to the appointment with me. During the company meeting, my mother sent me notes: "Roses are red, violets are blue; boy, Kent, have I got a surprise for you." Funny, huh? She was the only one laughing.

I told Kent that my mother and I were leaving the meeting in the afternoon because she needed to go to her doctor. And just like that, my pregnancy was confirmed. Even though I had known all along, having it confirmed devastated me all over again. It was just not a good time for me to be pregnant—businesswise, financially, and for me personally. Back at the meeting my mother began sending me notes again. No poems this time, just "You tell Kent today or I will."

On the way back from the meeting, I said to Kent, "I need you to go by the mall on the way home." He asked me why, and I said, "Just stop. Would you just stop at the mall? I need to get something!" By that point, Kent would do anything to avoid raising my hackles. We went into the mall, and I led us directly to the baby department. In the middle of the cribs, I stopped. "Kent, do you like this crib?" He looked at me like I'd lost my mind (which was possible).

He said, "I guess. Who's it for?"

I repeated myself, "Do you like this crib? Or do you like that one?"

"Well, I don't know," he said. "Who's it for?"

"It's for you. It's for us."

Kent just stood there, all the blood draining from his face. When he gathered himself, he said, "Okay, let's go have coffee." He was excited, which made me mad. I needed him to commiserate with me, or at least that's what I felt like I needed at the time.

When we got back to my mother's house, we took the boys into the bedroom and said, "Boys, we need to tell you something. There won't be four of us anymore."

Bryan piped up, excited. "Are we getting a dog?"

Kent told him no, which led Bryan to flop back on the bed and say, "I knew it. You're getting rid of me. I knew I was adopted."

Ray took one look at me and said, "No, Mom's going to have a baby." He just knew it instantly. That was that. Although I was still upset and conflicted about it, I was relieved. Sharing such a secret with the ones dearest to my heart was like releasing the valve on a pressure cooker; I could breathe again. I wasn't as excited as they all were about the news, but their excitement was contagious, and little by little I began to feel it too.

I did a lot of praying during that period in my life, and I'm grateful God honored my prayers and was merciful, because I sure could have messed that whole thing up. The four of us drove back home to Richardson the next day, and life went back to normal. The boys went to school and their activities, and Kent and I went back to building the business and our lives.

Jeff was born in June of 1981, and I stayed home with him for about six months. When I went back to work, I took Jeff with me. When he was about three, the Lord once again sent us the right people at the right time. We met a family that lived close to our office who welcomed Jeff into their home. They were like a natural extension of our family, and they treated Jeff like a member of theirs. It was a very casual and easy relationship. I could take Jeff early or pick him up early.

I could leave him five days one week and three days the following week. It was the perfect working solution, such a change from the difficult day care days with Ray and Bryan when they were young.

That difference was a big deal for me, because when my older boys were young and they were in day care, it always felt so hard. It seemed that either they didn't like the day care or I didn't, and I would have to find another one. When they were really young, it was difficult for me to leave them; I shed a lot of tears dropping them off. I had a lot of working-mom guilt back then.

There were other ways in which raising Jeff was made easier. I had two live-in babysitters now that Ray and Bryan were teenagers, and I was more willing to let go of some of my ideas of what was "right" that I had clung so fiercely to when my first two were growing up. I think this is true for a lot of parents with a growing family.

You might think having a "surprise" baby would be enough commotion for one year. But whether Kent and I were just foolish, stubborn, or a combination of the two, we chose to commit to our business in a big way. By this time, we owned and operated two franchise operations. The next level was a trainership, which meant selling and helping new franchises grow. By this time, we knew we wanted to help others buy and build their franchises too.

When we spoke to our corporate mentor and advisor, Herman, he said, "You know what? You two need to skip the trainership level and just go straight for the directorship." Herman made us write a five-year management plan to qualify us to spend a small fortune on this vague entity. Kent and I worked on the plan for weeks. We bled over it. We printed it on parchment paper and put it in a three-ring gold binder, sent it off to Herman, and waited anxiously. It came back with so many red lines through it I felt like I was back in high school. It made me mad and made me cry, but we were committed by then, so we did a rewrite. It was years later that we found out no one had ever had to write a plan before to get approved!

Herman accepted our revised plan and began the arduous task of trying to make something of us as directors. His passion, his demand for excellence, and his confidence has always been valuable. He saw potential in us and expected us to live up to it. Herman was the smartest person we knew, and we did what he told us. We signed a paper that said, "Go forth and sell franchises, and help them grow so that you and the brand will grow."

By December of 1981, only three years after having moved to Richardson, we bought our directorship with very little training—and a huge note to pay. We had a lot to learn. When I think back to those years, I understand why I felt so crazy all the time. Zig Ziglar once said, "It's okay to get upset, even to yell and scream; just go in your closet and do it, then come out and be calm." I spent a fair amount of time in my closet in those days.

It was one of our best decisions and enabled us to grow personally, provide even better for our family, and help change the lives of other families. But first, there was much work to be done.

THINGS TO CONSIDER

- Know there are people to help you through tough times. Be open to them.
- Change is tough but often moves you forward. Be brave.
- Surprises are sometimes your greatest blessing. Be grateful.
- Guilt is not helpful.
- Get a big closet!

CHAPTER 3

TWO SKIPPERS, ONE SHIP

When we jumped into the directorship, we became responsible for selling franchises and helping them grow and become financially stable. Fortunately, we had some experience selling franchises prior to acquiring the directorship. Our strong belief that this was a great business to be in had led us to help two of our employees establish their franchise while continuing to build our own. Through that experience, we realized that investing in and helping others succeed was something we wanted to do—it was part of who we were. I think that is what made us leap into the directorship option so quickly.

We didn't receive much training from corporate, so we learned as we went. In the first two years, we sold four or five franchises. As our direct business grew and we took on more responsibilities working with other franchises, which were primarily owned by couples, we began developing regular training seminars and retreats. Through those interactions, the franchisees shared the challenges they faced of being spouses *and* business partners. Common themes were debating who was the "real" owner, whose ideas and ways of doing things were the "right" way, and how money should be spent.

This was all too familiar to us, as we had been butting heads on these very same issues since we went into business together. It's one thing to be married. It's one thing to be in business for yourself. It's a whole new ball game when you're self-employed and your business partner is your spouse. Kent and I both have strong personalities—different, but strong. Once I came into the business, I believed I had the right to have 100 percent say in how things went. That didn't work out so well, because Kent also believed he had 100 percent say in how things went. We disagreed on how to spend money, how to deal with employees, and how to deal with customers—we disagreed on pretty much everything.

We struggled with identifying our individual roles. I'm conservative when it comes to money, and Kent knows it takes money to grow—this was always in contention. If Kent felt the business needed a new piece of equipment, he would buy it, and I would find out about it when the bill arrived. I'd get my hackles up and tell him we couldn't afford the new equipment. I had electric bills, phone bills, and payroll this week. He would counter, "We need that piece of equipment to grow the business."

Neither of us was wrong, but how we were going about it was. I was the one who usually gave in, but never without a fight, and that takes a toll on a business partnership and a marriage. Once we began working with other franchisees and hearing their same struggles, we knew we had to figure out how to make it work ourselves if we were truly going to help other franchise owners be successful, and so we embarked on a strengths-and-weakness exercise that helped us determine how two skippers could successfully steer one ship.

Being a visual person, I arranged for a time away from daily responsibilities, set up a flip chart, got different-colored markers out, and suggested we try to get everything on paper so we could look at it objectively. First, we made a list of every single activity each of us did on a daily or weekly basis. We included everything from making sales calls to getting haircuts—in other words, everything that consumed our time and energy in the business and in our personal life.

Then we made lists of our strengths—what each of us was good at and where we operated most comfortably and effectively. Next, we tackled our weaknesses—what we weren't good at or performed least effectively. Both lists were hard, but they gave clarification to some of the disagreements we were having. By this time, we had also realized that our disagreements weren't simply hard on us; our employees felt the dissension, too, leaving them confused and frustrated—which only served to send us all off course.

Now that we had identified our strengths, weaknesses, and preferences, we could determine which roles and responsibilities we should each assume. Kent always wanted to step into money management, but I was better at it. This exercise helped him see this more clearly, even though it was still hard for him to accept. Because I'm outgoing and get along well with people, Kent always wanted me to go out and help sell, but just the idea of going out and selling would send me to my closet for a good scream. Selling meant people would say no to you, they would reject you, and disappointment wasn't something I handled well.

Kent was much better at being upbeat and service minded. He was always willing to solve our customers' problems, even if they were in the wrong. Back then, I was firmly stuck in my "right is right and wrong is wrong" mindset—not the best tack to take in customer service. I worked hard on improving my tolerance and perspective over the years, and eventually I realized that most things in life are never black and white, and I was able to handle customer conflict in a way that was best for our customers and for our business.

Those were two huge issues, and once we agreed that I knew best about money and Kent knew best about selling, we decided that I would not continue to try to tell him how to sell or how he should deal with customers, and he wouldn't come in and say "I just bought $20,000 worth of equipment" without discussing and planning for it in advance.

We both accepted full responsibility for what we agreed to do and committed to stay in our own lanes.

There was one final exercise to complete. The last exercise we did was to go back to the very first flip chart page where we'd listed everything both of us did, focusing on the "golden hours" during the day that could be used to make our business successful. One of the questions we asked ourselves was this: "What on this list will have the greatest impact on our business?" The others were, "Who is the only person who can do it?" and "Does it have to be done during the golden hours?" Seeing this all on paper made us realize that we had fallen into a common bad habit: being busy but not accomplishing the most important things.

We highlighted those activities that had a significant impact on our business and could only be done during the golden hours. It was easy to see that sales were a critical activity, and that was Kent's most important job. The first things to get crossed off the list were activities like getting gas, getting haircuts, running to the bank, fixing equipment. It wasn't that these things didn't need to get done, but did we need to do them during those precious golden business hours? It was time to delete or delegate, then do what remained.

When deciding what needs to be done, there are three options: Delete it. Delegate it. Do it.

The activities that we determined did need to be done during regular business hours couldn't all be accomplished by Kent and me. Now we had to *delegate*. We looked at each activity and the skill set of our staff and determined who would now be responsible for those activities.

We knew this represented a significant change, not only for us but for our staff as well. They would have to learn new skills and take on more responsibility. There was grumbling when Kent held the staff meeting, but we forged on. We had to retrain ourselves, and we had to retrain our staff. It took time and the commitment to breaking old habits of how we had run the business—this process wasn't always easy or fun. Kent, being the obsessive person he is, did better than the rest of us. It was sometimes tempting to ask him to go do an estimate or tackle a piece of equipment. He stuck to his guns, though, and said he was just too busy doing *sales*.

> **When deciding what needs to be done, there are three options: Delete it. Delegate it. Do it.**

He now admits that he was having a great time and not working as hard as he had when he was doing production, estimates, fixing equipment, trying to solve everyone's problems, and being "Captain of the World." A year later, our volume had doubled, and everything that needed to get done got done.

The problem had been *us*. We'd focused on being busy and productive, but we weren't getting the results we wanted or needed. This exercise and following through with its outcomes helped us right our ship, but it also gave us the opportunity to share our struggles and how we worked through them with those we were entrusted to mentor. We were now able to provide franchise owners a tool with which to work through their own challenges of determining roles and responsibilities and provide them the ongoing coaching support to stick with it. If you have reached your plateau, I challenge you to go through this exercise and commit to spending your time doing what gets you the results you want.

We learned from our franchisees too. Kent was the one who left the house every day and faced customers and faced rejection. And while he did all that, I sat home in my protective cocoon—something I came to appreciate when mentoring one of our first franchise couples. The husband was talking to me about their struggles at home between personal and business. He told me that his wife was always saying she was going to quit, and that was a struggle for him. I didn't understand and asked what the struggle was. He said, "She always has the choice to quit. I never do." That was eye opening for me. I could quit (and I had), and I could sit home and grumble, but Kent would still have to go out every day and face rejection while always maintaining an optimistic, life-is-great attitude. That was a strength of his I had not appreciated enough.

Learning to appreciate each other's strengths and accept each other's weaknesses is a great lesson for both personal and professional relationships. The effort Kent and I put into learning how to work better together in the business carried over into our personal life—how we raised our boys, how we chose to live our life, and how we chose to deal with adversity—but that doesn't mean it was always easy.

You may not own a business with your partner, but the principles apply to relationships, running a home, and raising a family too.

THINGS TO CONSIDER

- There are three options to get things done: Delete it. Delegate it. Do it.
- Appreciate each other's strengths, and acknowledge weaknesses.
- Decide who's responsible for what, and then stay in your lane.
- Being busy doesn't mean you are accomplishing anything.

CHAPTER 4

I MARRIED A RISK TAKER

Dear Kathy, I don't want to see you. Don't come to campus. Don't make this harder than it is.

Those words devastated me. They also confused me. Where was this coming from?

I left college to go to work, because my parents didn't have the money to pay for college. My plan was to work for a while and save money to go back to school. On weekends, I either visited Kent at school, or he hitchhiked down to see me. It all seemed to be working well until, after visiting him one weekend, I received a "Dear Kathy" letter three days later. I had no idea what had transpired in his mind after I'd left that Sunday, but here I was reading the words that broke my heart. I cried for a month, only stopping after my mother threatened me.

Kent's letter also infuriated me. Who was he to tell me I couldn't come to campus? And why would he treat me this way? It was a new experience for me. I had always dated nice, respectful boys who followed the rules and did what was proper. Kent didn't follow the rules, and I decided that I didn't need that kind of trouble in my life, so although my heart was breaking, I never tried to contact Kent after I received his letter. I put my focus back into work and had finally begun dating again when one night my mother and I were startled awake at 1:00 a.m. by our ringing phone.

"I've made a mistake. I'm sorry. I don't know what I was thinking. I want to see you."

To hear him so upset after all the pain he had caused me made me a little happy, and it also strengthened my resolve to not just go running back to him no matter how badly I wanted to.

"Can I see you?" Kent pleaded.

"I don't know. I'm pretty busy," I said.

I was playing it cool, leaving me little to say on that call, but a couple of days later I received a very different letter than the one he had sent me two months before. This one was full of apologies and his admission that he'd made a mistake—he had gotten nervous by how serious we had gotten. As you will soon see, he had reason to be nervous!

Several weeks went by, and he called again to ask if he could come to see me. I agreed, and he took the three-hour bus ride to my hometown. Once I saw Kent, my resolve to play it cool lasted but a minute; I was still as crazy about him now as I'd been the first time I spied him walking across campus looking very much out of place. No one wore white jeans and white loafers after Labor Day in Texas! But Kent—tan, short dark hair, red-and-white-checked shirt with sleeves rolled up to reveal very tanned arms—wore them with confidence. Boy, did I think he was cute and definitely different.

In fact, Kent and I couldn't have been more different. He was from Hawaii, a whole different world from the conservative, follow-the-rules Texas I grew up in. It seemed so foreign to my family that my grandfather believed Hawaii wouldn't be around much longer. It was surely going to sink. Kent, on the other hand, never concerned himself with what others might think or if he didn't do things according to what was right. Follow the rules? Those didn't always apply to Kent. He did what he wanted, and it wasn't long before he decided that, at the end of the semester, he would go back to Hawaii to finish school, happily telling me that he would send for me. I could live with his parents and find a job.

That wasn't going to work for my conservative, rule-abiding self, but June was still three months away. I continued to work, and we planned for his parents' visit for Kent's brother's wedding. Time went by quickly, and before I knew it, Kent and I were singing the Hawaiian wedding song to Nathan and his new bride. It was a lovely and emotional ceremony, and it meant that in a week Kent would be returning to Hawaii with his family. Without me.

Later that evening, we were sitting in my mother's backyard, and Kent was talking excitedly about how he would send for me and how I could live with his parents, who would help me find a job and an apartment. I looked at him and said, "Kent, that's not going to work for me. I'm not willing to sit here and wait."

The reality of Kent's leaving had finally hit me. I didn't want him to be in Hawaii while I stayed in Texas, unable to date. Maybe I was still smarting from his recent desertion.

"Well, what are you talking about?" he asked.

I said, "We need to get married."

When Kent picked himself up off the ground and began breathing again, he agreed to marry me. (Still today, I can't believe he agreed.)

That was on a Monday night. I ran into the house and woke my mother. "Mom, what are you doing next Tuesday?"

"I don't know," she said. "Do you want to go shopping?"

"No," I said. "I think I'll get married."

Surprisingly, my mother, who didn't like surprises, never blinked an eye. She never questioned what we were doing. She just asked, "Is this what you want? Is this going to make you happy?"

This all had to happen in a week's time, as I intended to go back with Kent and his family the following week. Because we lived in a small town where everybody knew me and I had more grandparents, aunts, and uncles than anyone needs, we were able to pull off a full church wedding. I borrowed my cousin's wedding dress, and my mother's good friend took a week's vacation to alter the dress and make my trousseau.

You can imagine the rumors that flew when this little Southern Baptist goody two-shoes got married in a week. My mother had to deal with the gossip for a few months until it was obvious she wasn't going to be a grandmother anytime soon.

When I think of it now, I can see that I was taking some serious risks deciding so quickly to move so far from the only home I'd ever known, but at the time, it didn't feel risky to me. I guess I was just a sucker for Kent and would go wherever he went. Through the entire week of planning the wedding right up to the time my father and I walked into the church, I didn't have a single jitter. Kent was another story. He was still traumatized by this turn of events, so when I walked in the back door of that church, I turned to my father and said, "We have to hurry, or I think he's going to run."

The wedding went off without a hitch, and the next day we set off on our honeymoon in a car filled with my in-laws, Margaret and Oliver; Kent's six-year-old nephew; and a fifty-four-year-old man with disabilities whom my in-laws cared for. We drove from Texas to California, crossing the desert in June in a car with no air-conditioning. I fell forever in love with my mother-in-law. She took great care of us all on that long, unbearably hot ride, always ready with a cold cloth for our necks, and she made sure her son and his new bride, whenever possible, had the privacy they wanted.

The first night we checked into a hotel, my father-in-law asked for connecting rooms for all of us. My mother-in-law, who did not speak up to my father-in-law very often, said, "Oliver, we're not going to do that."

And he said, "Well, of course we are."

"No," she said. "You will get Kent and Kathy a room at the end of the hall."

We finally arrived in California a couple of days later, and off we all flew to Hawaii.

We lived with Margaret and Oliver at first. Kent got a job as a security guard with a hotel, and I tried hard to find a job. It was difficult, because I was only nineteen and didn't have any real work experience, and I was what the natives called a mainland Haole (Caucasian), so businesses were less than eager to hire me. I did finally land a job as a secretary for the managing partner of a plumbing supply house. The partner was also a Haole and was everyone's boss.

In order for me to get my job done, I needed to interact with others, but no one would speak to me. I'd stand at their desk to ask a question, and they would turn away and start talking to someone else. I had never been treated like that or seen anyone else treated like that.

He explained that locals resented mainland Haoles who came to the island and took their jobs. This was the first time I had personally experienced prejudice or, honestly, even knew it existed. It was an eye-opening experience for this small-town Texas girl.

After I'd been with the company a few months, another employee, a Japanese woman, came up to my desk and said, "Hey, you married to a local boy?"

"I am," I said.

"How come you not tell us?" she laughed.

"Because nobody asked," I said.

Being married to Kent was my golden ticket. Once you are accepted by these wonderful people, they will literally die for you. That initial struggle made me even more grateful for how welcoming and wonderful my in-laws were to me from the moment they met me.

For the next three years, Kent worked the night shift. I would go home after work, eat supper, and go visit him in the security booth until I couldn't keep my eyes open. Then I'd go back home, sleep a few hours, get up and go to work the next morning, and then do it all over again. Eventually, Kent joined his dad at the fire department in Honolulu, where Oliver was the assistant fire chief. It wasn't long after that I decided I was ready to start a family.

Kent and I had never really talked about having a family, but one day I just woke up and told Kent, "I'm ready." He agreed, and a month later I was pregnant. I went to the doctor by myself to confirm, and when I showed up at the fire station, Kent asked, "Did you come to have dinner with me?"

"No," I said with a smile. "I came to tell you that you're going to be a dad."

We were both thrilled, and Ray was born in September of 1966. Around the time Ray was a year old, it occurred to me that I might never live in Texas again. It wasn't that I was ever homesick or that I didn't love Hawaii, because I did, and I loved my in-laws, but when we left Texas, I hadn't thought that it might be forever. Now, as a parent, I began to consider whether this was where I wanted to raise my children. Kent and I began to talk about leaving the islands and where we would go.

Kent had no interest in spending the rest of his life in Hawaii and, like me, didn't want to raise our children there. We talked about the West Coast, but we eventually settled on Texas. It was my home and a place that Kent loved.

Kent's brother was in Fort Worth at the time, so in January Kent moved in with his brother in his small, two-bedroom apartment, and Ray and I joined them in March. Before we left, we sold everything we had except for thirty-six boxes of clothes and toys and household goods, which we had shipped over. And so began our life in Fort Worth. It was a challenging time. Kent was busy looking for work, and I was home with Ray, and just a few months after we arrived, Oliver died suddenly of a heart attack. It was a tremendous loss for all of us, and within a month of losing Oliver, Margaret was diagnosed with cancer.

They had both been such a loving and supportive presence for us, and now we were more than three thousand miles away from Margaret. It was an incredibly painful time in our young lives, but somehow life continued to propel us forward.

Kent found work, and luckily it wasn't long before we found a house to rent. By then I was pregnant with Bryan, and just before he was born, we bought a huge, double-wide mobile home that was big enough for everything we needed. We moved that home around a couple of times, eventually finding our way to Houston, buying our first real home and starting a business.

In the first five years of being married to Kent, we moved five times. We'd both left jobs with no new job to go to, even after we had become parents! Those choices were not something I would have ever imagined I would make—my sense of stability and security seemed to be out the window, and I couldn't even say Kent made me do it, because as I look back, it was me who willingly took the risk of moving three thousand miles away from home with my new husband, me who proposed we get married in the first place, and me who first suggested we move back to the mainland with a baby and no job. Maybe Kent married a risk taker too?

Perception is a funny thing, isn't it? I never thought of myself as a risk taker, but now, as I look back—and I don't know if this is a good admission or not—I think my being conservative and averse to what I considered risks was more about trying to do the right thing for the right reason. It was about desperately trying to not be embarrassed, to not look foolish, to not do anything that would upset somebody else. I was taught that children were seen and not heard. You dressed properly and spoke properly, and above all else, you followed the rules and did everything you were supposed to do, the way you were supposed to do it.

> **I think my being conservative and averse to what I considered risks was more about trying to do the right thing for the right reason.**

While I was clearly willing to take what others would consider significant risks, my desperate need to follow "the rules" and to not look foolish would be a battle that I would fight for many more years. The right way to raise our boys was a never-ending struggle. Kent was a rule breaker, concerned more about having fun than making sure the boys did what they were supposed to do. I resented his cavalier attitude and felt that he never took enough responsibility. He never worried about what the house looked like or if the boys broke a few rules.

Mice could have been munching on Fritos strewn across Ray's and Bryan's bedroom floors, and Kent wouldn't have been bothered a bit. When the police showed up at our door one day because Ray had been caught riding his dirt bike on private property (I had argued against getting the dirt bikes in the first place—see, I was right!), neither Kent nor Ray were the least bit upset. Ray was a minor and had no license, so it was Kent who got the ticket. Our son riding on private property and Kent receiving a ticket for it didn't sit well with me, and that they were both so casual about breaking these rules only served to upset me more.

At some point, when Bryan and Ray were preteens, I remember looking around and thinking, *Everyone is having fun except me*. I was the only one who was always upset, and it was exhausting. My mother was also a "right is right and wrong is wrong" person and was always upset about something. I could see myself at a crossroads.

Fortunately, I had wonderful girlfriends who guided me along a path of silliness that taught me to not take myself or life so seriously. I am forever grateful to all the wonderful women in my life who taught me how to let go and just laugh.

THINGS TO CONSIDER

- Sometimes love requires a leap of faith.
- Rules are important, but they are not everything, and trying to adhere to them all is exhausting.
- Learn to laugh along the way. Humor goes a long way to reducing stress.
- Don't sweat the small stuff—and really, most of it is small stuff!

PART II

LESSONS ALONG THE WAY

Seek out and value all the lessons family, friends, life, and God provide you. Learn from them, and never stop learning and growing as a person. I know I am. I've learned to laugh more and to focus on what is really important—there is more to life than making sure you follow all the rules! I've learned to let my children grow up. Trust me, you will like them even better as adults and friends. Our surprise child enabled my retirement and was greatly responsible for me writing this book. Who knew?

Experience isn't just a noun. It's also a verb that implies action, engagement. Friendships, laughter, and people in general make for great experiences, but you might miss out on the best part if you don't fully engage. My precious

> **As you are experiencing life, it's important to consider why you work, why you do what you do, and how to align that with your values.**

friends taught me how to fully engage in experiences along life's journey.

Leadership also requires engagement so you can grow from each experience and learn the lessons that result. It requires making tough decisions and accepting responsibility for those decisions. It's about the ability to admit mistakes and learn from them. It's knowing your values and living them as an example to those you lead.

As you are experiencing life, it's important to consider *why* you work, *why* you do what you do, and how to align that with your values.

The lessons that follow, and many more not included, were important to growing up.

CHAPTER 5

LEARNING TO LAUGH

It was someone's fortieth birthday, and I was smart enough to know that my friends would not let me get away with wearing something normal or proper. I prepared. I scoured the thrift shop and was rewarded for my efforts with the ugliest long black dress I had ever seen and a pair of black clunky shoes. I was quite proud of myself that evening as I pulled on my long black gloves and set my grandmother's wide-brimmed black hat on my head. I glanced in the mirror. Something was missing. I grabbed all the gold chains I had, and I rubbed an abundance of pink rouge to my cheeks. I was ready. This was the new Kathy, one that could walk into a restaurant ridiculously dressed and not be embarrassed—well, maybe I would still feel embarrassed, but I no longer let that stop me from doing something fun.

My entrance was met with surprise and peals of laughter. While everyone was also decked out in black, I was the most outrageously dressed, and my friends were all so proud of me! Who said I couldn't be spontaneous and fun?

This wonderful group of women, who became lifelong friends, had reached out to me when I volunteered as my youngest son's first-grade room mother. After our first meeting, I got a call from one of them asking if I wanted to join them for dinner once a month. I didn't know them, and it seemed evident they were already friends. I was hesitant but didn't want to seem rude, so I agreed. It didn't take me long to figure out that these women were bent on embarrassing themselves and having an enormously good time at it. It was never just dinner—their creativity for nonsense was boundless.

For one birthday we went to a nice restaurant dressed as clowns. Our friend was frightened of clowns. Such friends! Another time one of them took a fall from her bicycle. The next time we met, we showed up at the restaurant on tricycles to surprise her. We even strapped yellow tennis balls to our heads to emulate her bruised profile. You cannot imagine what a huge step this was for me. I hadn't quite shed enough of the conservative me and still worried: *What if someone from the school saw me? Worse, what if someone I knew from church or business was at the restaurant?*

Life marched on whether I had fun or not, so why wasn't I having more fun?

It was a revelation to me that I could be this ridiculous, this embarrassing, and yet the world did not collapse around me—life marched on whether I had fun or not, so why wasn't I having more fun?

After a few years of friendship, I asked what had made them ask me to join their little group. "Oh my, we could see that you needed to lighten up!"

God sent more wonderful women into my life over time, each one of them offering life lessons to guide me. Shortly after Kent and I went into business, we made a trip to New England to garner experience and knowledge from those who had been at it longer. Here, I met another lifelong friend. Judy had a heart for everyone and never met a stranger. She carried snacks and water in her car to give to people on the street. She played practical jokes on everyone and offended no one. She was also honest. She once told me that people were hesitant to approach me because I was very intimidating. I was surprised and maybe a little offended. I asked, "What is it that I do? I mean, you don't look at me that way, do you?"

"No," she said, smiling. "Because I learned to laugh at you first. But to be a friend of others, you have to let them be a friend to you. You're so independent and self-assured that people think you don't need anything, not even a friend. If you can't ever ask something of them, they will not feel free to ask anything of you."

> **But to be a friend of others, you have to let them be a friend to you.**

I had never intended to come across as intimidating and may never have realized I was if Judy hadn't been straightforward with me. I had learned with Kent that being partners required you to let the other person see your weaknesses and your needs, and now I had to work on applying that same practice to my friendships as well.

It was a good lesson on the two faces of friendship, a lesson that taught me to let down my guard and let people in. Judy and I traveled together, laughed together, and cried together over the years. Through her friendship, I learned what it means to truly love people and enjoy life. Judy made everyone feel loved and welcome, and I strive to pass that gift along. She went to be with the Lord several years ago, and I sometimes imagine I hear her laughing in heaven.

I would have been fully blessed to have had only these girlfriends, but I was fortunate to befriend more wonderful women along the way. Meeting new people was one of the many blessings of our business.

At a conference in Hawaii, a corporate staff member asked if we would have lunch with a couple from California who were considering becoming trainers. We had a nice visit, and they did eventually increase their involvement in the business, but that wasn't the best part! As they walked away that day, I told Kent, "You will think I'm crazy, but that young woman is going to be a part of my life."

We have been friends for over thirty years. DeeDee and I travel together, share our fears and our joys, celebrate our families, and, of course, laugh a lot. At one point in our friendship, I honored the lesson that Judy taught me and reached out to two other Texas girls along the way, inviting them to join DeeDee and me on our travels. What a wonderful gift Cindy and Susan have been. We try to see each other several times a year, and our text chains are frequent and hilarious.

These friends have taught me about faith, friendship, fun, and laughter. After we had traveled together a few times, DeeDee said one day, "Boy, people just don't know how amiable you can really be." This was one more true friend telling me I needed to lighten up. I think I have finally gotten the message, although I'm a work in progress. I still have moments when I let my need to have things be "right" overshadow my ability to just let the little things go and have fun. But I recognize it now and can work more quickly to adjust my perspective.

If you don't have girlfriends that tell you the truth and make you laugh, get some as soon as you can.

The best girlfriends don't make demands on each other, and I found that the release of not having to worry about making everyone else happy all the time or worrying about letting anyone down makes them the best travel companions of all—and I love traveling! Yes, I enjoy traveling with Kent, but it's not the same. He has a lot of expectations. He's happy if I go along with him, and sometimes he's happy to go along with me, but in the end, he's what I call a *destination traveler.*

With my girlfriends, it's not all about the destination—it's about enjoying everything along the way. We are *experience travelers*. Everything is an experience. Everything is funny. Everything has a story. Everything is a remembrance. We free ourselves from expectations. Traveling with DeeDee is a perfect example of this. DeeDee's idea of going to a museum, even one as extraordinary and world renowned as the Louvre, is to walk in the front door, stay five minutes, and then say, "I'm done." I have no intention of leaving there until they kick me out, but those differences don't matter, because when DeeDee is done, she'll just say, "I'm going back to the hotel. See y'all there." Those of us who want to stay reply "See you there" and don't feel any guilt over whether we should stay or go. We simply do what we would like to do while respecting what the others want to do.

I think we are able to allow ourselves and each other this gift because we've all worked so hard, we've all raised families together, we know what we've all been through, and we know what it took to make it through it all. When we travel, we give ourselves complete freedom to have a good time.

I love traveling to places I've never been before, and while I think I would have always enjoyed travel, I'm not sure I would have been quite so enamored with it if I hadn't experienced so much of it with girlfriends. They have expanded my horizons in ways I would never have been able to do on my own or with Kent. If I had not witnessed DeeDee on so many occasions walk up to someone in a foreign country and start speaking to them in English, a language they did not understand, and see them reply in their language, one that DeeDee did not understand, and DeeDee always end up hugging them and kissing them on the cheek, I would probably never have been brave enough to speak to someone who didn't speak English, because I was always so afraid to be embarrassed by my inability to clearly communicate with them.

But not DeeDee. She'd return from her animated conversations, and I would ask, "What did y'all talk about?"

"Oh, I don't know," she'd say. "But weren't they wonderful?" Seeing DeeDee in action helped me set my fear of embarrassment aside and realize that most people, if you try to communicate with them, appreciate it and respond positively.

All the lessons I learned from my girlfriends translated beyond my role as friend. They made me a more empathetic listener and communicator as a mother, wife, and business leader.

THINGS TO CONSIDER

- If you don't have girlfriends, get some as soon as possible.
- Don't wait for friends to come along! Reach out to others, and invite them to join you.
- Remember to offer help *and* request help—friendship works both ways.
- Be silly often!
- No one ever died of embarrassment.
- Trust friends, and let them help you grow.
- Watch for those people God sends you throughout your life.
- People everywhere are wonderful—take chances with them.
- Become an "experience" traveler.

CHAPTER 6

LEARNING TO LEAD

No matter your perspective, whether you're an employee, employer, mentor, or mentee, we all have to make choices and accept the responsibility for those choices. Shortly after embarking on our directorship and selling our last franchise, I quickly realized that the responsibility for those choices is far greater when you are the one leading the way.

About six months after we had taken on the directorship and sold our last franchise, its owner came to us and said, "You can buy this business back right now, or you can say no and in six months I'll have run it into the ground, and you can have what's left."

The franchise was already a mess, and we needed to take ownership before it became unsalvageable. The owner had run off all the employees except for one,

We all have to make choices and accept the responsibility for those choices.

a guy who had worked for us previously. The day after we took back ownership, Kent was seeing customers, something he hadn't done for years, and I was in the office when the one remaining employee walked in and asked if he and I could talk. "Of course," I said.

"I drew up a contract," he began.

"That's interesting. I thought I wrote up the employment contracts," I said.

"Not this one."

At that time, we had a percentage program for employees: rather than paying them hourly or on salary, they received 30 percent of the revenue of each job and the company received 70 percent. With that 70 percent, the company paid all the expenses. In his contract, it was reversed. The company would get 30 percent and he would get 70 percent.

I said, "Okay, I can agree to that."

He was surprised that I had agreed so quickly. "Good," he said.

"You know that with 70 percent comes all the expenses. You'll be responsible to pay all rent, taxes, insurance, vehicle payments, and all the products that you use."

"Oh no, no, no," he said. "That's not part of my contract."

It was truth time. If Kent and I were to successfully lead our franchisees, we would have to make some tough decisions. Being in business for ourselves definitely had its benefits, but it also meant that we were solely responsible for its success or failure. It's easy to take the credit when things go well; it's a lot harder when things don't go right to say "I've got to do something different" or "I've got to work harder" or "I've got to make better decisions." And it was time to make the decision that Kent and I were going to have to work harder for a while.

If I let the employee go, it meant Kent and I *were* the employees, but if I took his contract, what type of leadership example would we be setting? I said, "You've been a good employee, but what you're proposing is not acceptable to the company. It's not financially feasible for the company, but more importantly, you're not living the value, respect, and family system that we have. You can leave your keys on my desk and your uniform at the door."

Now came the most difficult part—calling Kent and telling him that the jobs he was selling were jobs he would have to service. I had made a choice to stick to our value system, which meant Kent and I had to suck it up and do the hard stuff. We rebuilt that franchise and owned it for three years before we sold it again. It wasn't easy, but we survived. You can change your choices, but don't do it foolishly, because once you make one choice, there are lots of others, both good and bad, that will come along as consequences of that choice.

Kent and I chose to stick to our value system throughout our time in business:

Customer service is priority number one.

The customer is always right—even when they're not.

Treat employees and customers with respect, and take the time to listen to what they really need.

Provide adequate training: you can't hire somebody today and throw them out there with a customer tomorrow and assume they know what you value or how they should treat the customer.

We required our employees to adhere to these values while on the job. Employees needed to choose to show up on time and be respectful of their fellow employees and our customers. They had to accept that the customer was always right. They had the right to disagree, but if they chose to work for us, they had a responsibility to uphold this code even when they didn't agree, and we had a responsibility to provide them the training, resources, and support to do their job well.

It's been my experience that most people want to do their job well when given the tools and training to do so. Perhaps more importantly, the employee needs to know how their employer thinks. They need to understand what their employer's values are—not just what their employers do but *why* they do it. We tried to make sure our employees understood our expectations and values, and as the employer, we did our best to set a consistent example. Sometimes we missed the mark.

During one particular call, the adjuster told me the client he was referring to us was trouble and was going to be difficult. I mentioned this to my assistant, who then relayed that information to the production crew assigned to the job. When the crew returned, they wouldn't stop complaining about how difficult she was, how picky she was, how she watched everything they did.

I spoke up. "Wait a minute. Our value is that the customer is always right. And y'all are taking this stand that this customer is a problem."

The employee turned to me and said, "Well, you told us she was."

That stopped me in my tracks. They were right. It was a great lesson for me. I couldn't speak my values and hold my employees to them and then not act out those values. I think that's a real struggle for most of us, whether we're at work or at home or within our relationships. We don't do it intentionally, but it's hard to always stay true to standards we've set for ourselves and others. You can't tell your children not to complain about teachers and school and then let them hear you complain about work. Matching your actions to your values is hard, but it's so important to keep trying.

I acknowledged my mistake and called the customer to see what her concerns were. Her issue was that she had just been through the trauma of having her house on fire and her personal possessions damaged. She was worried about further loss should our crew break or steal anything. I better understood where she was coming from, and to make things right, it just took my production manager going the next day and saying to her, "Before we start, I'd like to sit down with you and give you more information about exactly what we're going to do, how long we're going to be here, and that we're here to answer any questions you have." She just needed reassurance. She wasn't difficult at all. She was a very good customer who in the end gave us a great recommendation.

We changed our perspective and process as a result. Our staff no longer went in "to clean up a mess"; they went in with the perspective that they were providing a service to someone who was in a difficult situation. It was a huge lesson in taking time to understand the customer's perspective, especially in the event of a disaster.

A few years later I was my own difficult customer in a time that provided another level of understanding, one that I would end up sharing with our franchisees many times.

Kent and I were away for a few days when we got a call from our son. "Mom, I hate to tell you this, but you have a problem. Your hot water heater exploded, and your house is flooded." The entire first floor was under water. All our furniture had to be moved out so the floors and cabinets could be replaced, walls repainted, and furniture refinished. We lived in a rental for six months and incurred a $150,000 loss. It was a big deal.

Once the repairs were made and my furniture was returned, I noticed there were only six dining room chairs around my large table instead of eight. I called and said, "I think you misplaced two of my chairs. I only have six." The young man politely said that he would check for me. He then called back to say he was sorry, but the missing chairs weren't in the warehouse. I instructed him to call the refinisher to see if they were there; I wanted my chairs found. This went back and forth a few times until someone finally had the courage to call and say, "We've checked our videos. We only picked up six chairs from your house." This didn't make sense to me. Where were my two missing chairs?

I called my daughter-in-law, who'd helped me decorate my home, and said, "Kerri, I'm frustrated. I'm missing two chairs, and they are insisting they only picked up six, but I had eight."

"Oh no," she said. "You only had six. I always said that I thought you should have eight."

Now I had to call and confess that the chairs I'd insisted they find didn't exist. I was embarrassed, and I don't like to be embarrassed, but I took the opportunity not just to use this lesson for myself and our business but to share it with franchisees we mentored so they, too, could learn from it. They made great fun of me every time I told it, but it was important that I did.

The story helped us all see how easy it is for a customer, even one as organized as I was, to be confused or highly concerned in this type of situation, and it underscored the importance of doing our best to see it from the customer's perspective and then go a step further to improve the experience.

We always believed that if we did what we said we would do and the customer paid what they said they would pay, we were, at best, even. We taught our staff to look for something extra to do—something that was not in our estimate of work. It didn't have to be something big. In most cases, our customers' homes were in some form of disaster. They were inconvenienced, dealing with many details, and had a strange crew in their homes, sometimes for several days. We asked our crews to look for opportunities to clean out the ashes in a fireplace or wash dishes in the sink—simple things that made a big difference to our customers. The challenge was getting employees to see the value in doing this. It took repetition, follow-up, and support.

We found that recognition was an appreciated and effective form of support. I was often too bottom line, asking only surface questions when the crew returned. "Was the customer happy? Did you collect payment?" I had to learn to ask better questions, like "What did the customer tell you at the end of the job? What did you need that you didn't have to do your job well? How did your customer respond to you doing extra things for them? What was the hardest part of the job for you?"

These questions gave me insights into not only our customers but also how our employees approached their job and what their motivation and skills were. It also provided me the opportunity to recognize them for those things they did well. I learned the value in appreciating our employees more. I learned to spend more time just listening and asking questions about their lives outside of work. "What are your plans for the weekend? How are the kids doing in school? What sports do they play?" It took discipline to make the effort—not because I didn't care about what was going on with everyone but because, with so many demands on my time, I was already stretched thin. But it was important to make the effort. A trusted and loyal employee is always worth investing time and energy in.

Through this process, I realized that being independent didn't mean always being right. It also didn't mean always getting things done by myself. By listening more, I recognized that others' views and insights were helpful, added to my own value, and lessened my stress. I began to more actively look for ways to encourage and build others up in all aspects of my life. I benefited from the experience as much as those I encouraged.

You may not own your own business or be a supervisor or an employee. Hopefully some of these lessons can be applied well to other areas of your life. We are faced with hard decisions every day, and we are all leaders somewhere, to someone.

THINGS TO CONSIDER

- There are rewards and consequences for all choices—be prepared to accept both.
- Change is almost always hard—and scary. Don't let fear hold you back.
- Keep going! Things will look better in your rearview mirror and make great stories someday.
- Careful what you do and say; people are listening and watching you.
- Learn to see others' perspectives.
- Trust and invest in people.
- Assure your actions match your stated values.
- It's what you do beyond the expected that sets you apart from everyone else.

CHAPTER 7

MONEY AND MATTERS OF THE HEART

Money is a tool, not a purpose. If you don't know why you get up every morning and do what you do, why you work so hard, what you want to achieve, then what is the point, and how long can you convince yourself that you are happy doing it? This is a concept Kent and I put a lot of focus on in our retreats. Owning your own business is hard work, it can be thankless work, and its success or failure sits solidly on your shoulders. So why do we do it? By the way, this applies to any work you are doing.

I remember one particular couples retreat when I was really pushing one of our franchisees for his *why*.

"Why do you keep working so hard?" I asked.

"Because I need to make money," he said.

"Why do you need to make money?"

"Because we need to live in Dallas, and it's expensive."

"You don't need to live in Dallas," I countered. "You could move somewhere less expensive."

"But I still need a house for my family."

"You don't need a house," I countered. "You could be homeless. So, what is the real reason you work so hard?"

"Because I want to take care of my family."

"Why?"

"Because I love my wife, and I want to make life better for her."

"Why?" I continued to prod.

And with tears streaming down his face, his final response was this: "Because when I married her, I told her I would spend my life doing everything in my power to make her happy."

> **Money isn't the why. It's matters of the heart that provide the motivation for each of us to get up and do the hard stuff every day.**

Money isn't the *why*. It's matters of the heart that provide the motivation for each of us to get up and do the hard stuff every day. When Kent and I could get our franchisees to see that owning a business and working hard have to be about more than sending an invoice out and getting a check in return—that they have to be about something they want more than life itself—that's when we felt we had succeeded.

Before we could share this insight with our franchisees, Kent and I had to come to this realization for ourselves. When we first started out, we didn't think that way. We just thought about paying tomorrow's bills, the mortgage, and hopefully the electric bill. We bought equipment and vehicles and had office space and hired help—growing a business takes a lot of money, and we focused on making money to pay for all of it. A few years into this cycle, I began to realize that everything had become about the money, it wasn't very rewarding, and we weren't having much fun.

Then we heard Lou Tice speak on the topic of our subconscious and how it works, and that talk changed our lives.

Our company was big on motivational events with speakers like Tony Robbins and Zig Ziglar. They pulled us into how we could be successful and live the life of our dreams. We'd walk away on cloud nine. Then we'd get home, and there would be bills to pay, collections to make, employees who quit, a wrecked company van, and on and on.

We'd leave the convention on such a high, and within twenty-four hours of returning home I'd be depressed. It was all just hype that sounded great but didn't translate to our life.

When Lou Tice, founder of the Seattle-based Pacific Institute and self-help mentor, spoke at one of the conventions, he made sense. He spoke about the subconscious, saying that if we tell our subconscious we want to do something, like write a book, the subconscious believes that is what you want to do and sets that idea in motion. I'm a realist—I need concrete examples, and that made sense to me. I now understood the power of the subconscious and that it is the source of our habits. I no longer thought of it as just hype. The subconscious doesn't know if it's real or not. It doesn't know if you are serious or just kidding. It just sets about helping make it happen.

> Remember that plan our mentor, Herman, made us write when we first became directors? Well, many years later, we came across our plan, and not only had we completed everything in it, we had exceeded it in almost every area. All without even looking at it

> every day. We wrote it, we believed it, Herman expected it, our subconscious thought we were serious, and it worked. We have asked ourselves many times, How much more might we have accomplished, and how much faster, if we had been referring back to it all along?
>
> What you put into your mind and believe in will come to pass. Choose carefully what you put into your mind! Your subconscious takes you seriously regardless!

Kent and I began to really think through the importance of goal setting and management processes. We no longer saw money as the goal but as a tool to reach our goals and to fulfill our *why*—which for us was faith, family, friends, and to be able to be charitable in an impactful way. We began to live our belief that if you're doing the right thing for the right reasons personally or in business—but especially as it relates to money in business—if you're following procedures, if you have processes in place and you practice good management, if you provide quality service to your customers and go beyond what's required, and if you are prudent with your money—then the money comes as a result of all those efforts.

We didn't figure this all out overnight or by ourselves; we had lots of input from speakers over the years, and I value every single one of them. Zig Ziglar went to our church. We knew him personally and admired him. Maxwell Maltz, whose 1960 book, *Psycho-Cybernetics: A New Way to Get More Living Out of Life*, is considered the forerunner of the now popular self-help books. And, of course, Lou Tice, who helped me see why it works.

Once I understood it, I decided that we should try to fool our subconscious all the time. What really brought it home for me was a story Lou Tice told about an orphanage and a pool.

Lou and his wife were on the board of an orphanage. At every board meeting the desire to have a pool for the kids came up, but it was never put in the budget. Time and time again it would come up: "We really ought to visit the idea of a swimming pool. The kids would love it." And time and time again it would get tabled because no one believed they could ever afford it.

Then at one meeting, a new young board member said, "We need a free swimming pool." Everyone laughed. "No, really," he went on. "We need to find a way to get a pool that doesn't have to be paid for through the orphanage's budget." This was met with another round of laughter.

And then someone said, "You know, I know a guy with a backhoe who would be willing to help." Someone else said, "I know someone who would donate cement." Before they knew it, the children in the orphanage had a beautiful Olympic-sized pool. Not one penny came out of the budget, because every board member knew someone who could lend a hand.

I thought, *What a powerful story. If we all lived every day like that, imagine what we could accomplish.* That same year, Jeff was graduating from kindergarten and Bryan was graduating from high school. They both thought it would be cool to have a swimming party to celebrate.

We did not have a pool, so I said to Kent, "We need a swimming pool."

"I don't think that's going to happen," he said.

I had someone come out and give us an estimate. It was no surprise that it was over our budget. Kent said, "There's only one way for us to get a pool, and that's to finance one."

At the time, we were on a very serious debt-free plan, and I said, "No financing."

"Well, then no pool."

I didn't accept that. I told him that we were going to have a pool and that as the creator of income, he needed to go out there and book more jobs to create enough extra income. And he did. By the time Jeff and Bryan graduated, we had a pool with a fence and beautiful landscaping—all of it paid for with cash. Not one penny came out of our budget, because we thought about it and committed to it, and Kent worked really hard to bring in more sales. After a couple of months of enjoying the pool, I looked at him and said, "Could you do that again?"

"Not every day," he said. "But, yes, I could do it again." It felt good to prove to ourselves that we could envision this seemingly unattainable goal and make it happen. Seeing our boys enjoy that pool for many years made all the hard work worth it. It fulfilled our *why*. Being able to share this experience with our franchisees was invaluable—it wasn't just talk. Living what we taught in the retreats made them more powerful.

Many of our franchisees were struggling with the same things Kent and I struggled with. How do you run a business, be a family, be a husband and wife, manage money—it all gets so complicated. I thought, *Let's just talk about it*. Let's acknowledge how overwhelming the reality of disagreeing with each other is, and when you try to talk about it, the phone's ringing, the crew hasn't shown up for a job, and bills are due that you can't pay, and don't forget … you still need somebody to be upbeat and happy and go selling all the time. On top of all that day-to-day struggle, you have to keep your long-term vision and goals in mind, because if you lose sight of your why—why you get up every day and work so hard—you won't last. Not happily, anyway.

Our first couples retreat was on a Saturday night with four couples. We set an agenda of topics to cover—these were planned as productive conversations and exercises, not a gripe session. We also made sure we had some lighthearted fun. Thankfully, it was a success. Everyone felt comfortable sharing their experiences, and we really had a good time—and we now had a template on which to build future retreats. As we grew our directorship, we encouraged all our franchisees to take part in our retreats. Focus and hard work were always key themes in our retreats, but we also always incorporated fun.

One year we did a Mardi Gras theme, and everyone came in costume. We did mystery dinner theaters, boat parties, and all sorts of fun experiences. For Kent and me, motivating people to be engaged, work hard, and learn to balance these with fun was the best part. Life can be hard. Being in business for yourself is tough. And we saw early on that feeling you're a part of a larger group can help lift you up.

Eventually, I went on to present women's workshops at the national convention. Some of the wives were partners in the business while others had their own separate careers. The women's workshop focused on ideas for how to best manage it all and let them know that they were not alone; we all were facing the same challenges and trying to figure it out. I shared with them how Kent and I worked hard to keep our shared goals front and center, especially when things got hard. We'd remind ourselves that we wanted to provide security for our family, build a foundation for their future, maintain our faith, and stay married. This last one was key, because if your mindset is *If this marriage or business gets too hard, I'm just going to leave*, you can't remain motivated and committed to making it work.

Providing these women the tools that enabled them to figure out what they could agree on with their husbands, what their shared goals were, and what they wanted for their life helped them see that all the challenges were solvable. Soon after, we invited the guys to join us.

And so began our couples workshops at conventions for several years while continuing the retreats for our own franchisees throughout the duration of our directorship. Through our directorship, conventions, and retreats, we made wonderful lifelong friends who continue to sustain and expand our why, and we are better because of them.

My girlfriends and I were in Positano, Italy, several years back. One evening we were standing out on the balcony of our hotel taking in the view of this beautiful Italian village on the hillside and the ocean ebbing and flowing along its shores. It was everything you think you would ever want to see. We were talking about home, because even though we traveled a lot, we always worried about our businesses and families back home. I turned to my girlfriends and said, "Okay, we need to remember this magnificent view, this wonderful moment that we are all in together, and remember that this is why we do the hard stuff."

We have to know our why *and* find the moments to remind ourselves and celebrate our whys when they happen.

THINGS TO CONSIDER

- Real independence comes when you make choices that better align with your values and goals in life.
- Circumstances don't have to dictate your future.
- Choose to improve yourself and your circumstances; it is always up to you.
- Define your values and goals, and frequently remind yourself of what they are.
- Fool your subconscious—you'll be amazed at what dreams you can make come true.
- Work hard and have fun.
- Knowing your own personal *why* is critical.

PART III

A LIVING LEGACY

We all have stories. Stories that can serve to teach, entertain, and inspire. The stories of my life have been filled by those who have inspired and influenced me and by all the joyful, sorrowful, exciting, and challenging experiences that have shaped who I am. My two youngest granddaughters always beg me to tell my stories. It doesn't matter that they've heard them before, and sometimes they even correct me if I recite it differently from one telling to the next. Our family stories serve to connect them to the past and the future.

My hope is that you may be entertained and encouraged by the stories that follow. More importantly, I hope you will be inspired to tell and even write your own stories. Stories are what connect us. Each story is part of who you are and what those who are listening will remember. My story isn't finished yet. Neither is yours.

CHAPTER 8

FAMILY IS EVERYTHING

Kent and I have been through some crazy times over the last fifty-plus years together. We've moved more times than I can count, started over, took chances that made our families question our sanity, worked hard, and pushed ourselves to always do better. All of it—everything we did, crazy or not—we did to improve life for our family. For us, family is everything.

We've been fortunate to be able to blend our work and family life. Ray and Bryan grew up when we were struggling to first build the business, and Jeff grew up as the business expanded beyond our expectations. All three of the boys have been in the business for themselves, and so yes, we still talk business around the dinner table. I've been asked many times, "How do you do it? You all live so close and work together and always get along."

To which I reply, "Yes, we live close, and we work together, but I promise you, we do *not* always get along."

We disagree plenty, we get angry, and we sometimes say things we don't mean, but none of those things stand a chance against the love, encouragement, tears, forgiveness, strength, joy, faith, and laughter we give to one another.

Kent and I grew up in families that offered those same gifts. We've been blessed beyond measure with extended family—our own parents, grandparents, brothers, sisters, aunts, and uncles—and now we are blessed with our growing family, three wonderful daughters-in-law, nine perfect grandchildren, and a beautiful newborn great-grandson. The gifts they have all given us could fill a book on their own, so I will only share a few that show just how blessed I have been.

SISTERHOOD

I have a sister, Jean, six years younger. We weren't the best of friends growing up. I was bossy, and she was a brat. We've spent our adult years making up for it with lots of great adventures, but we agree our favorite was in Kenya, Africa, in 2014. We fell in love with Africa and its people, the landscape, and wild animals. One evening we were in our luxurious canvas tent when two young African men came to "close up" for us. Rain was expected that evening. We loved the large canvas openings and didn't want to "close up" just yet. Outside our tent was a deep chasm with tall trees in it filled with lively chattering monkeys, and we were enjoying watching them. The young men were fairly insistent, but we assured them we could handle canvas and zippers. It wasn't long before the storm arrived with a vengeance and we were quickly scurrying to secure the canvas in place. Heavy pelting rain and extremely strong winds assaulted us on all sides. The largest canvas window was six feet high and six feet wide. The heavy flap hung down, so it had to be lifted and zipped up on two sides and the top. Surprise! We couldn't handle it! We actually felt as if the entire tent would be blown away with us in it. My four-foot-eleven sister stood on a chair trying to lift and zip the flap while I held on to her backside to keep the wind from blowing her over. Water cascaded over both of us in a torrent. Our normal reaction to such situations kicked in—we began laughing hysterically, making everything even harder. We were now soaked, cold, and blown to pieces. By the time we got everything closed up, we were exhausted … as much from laughing as from the struggle. We sopped up as much water as possible from the floor, completely changed our clothes, and slipped into bed, where we slept peacefully through the rest of the storm.

Early the next morning, Jean woke me by calling me to the front door of our tent. That twenty-foot chasm was completely filled, with water rushing over the treetops, the rim, and within a couple of feet of the entrance to our tent. No sign of monkeys. They had obviously been smart enough to "close up" and get out of there early.

Each day we went on safari early in the morning, early afternoon, and at sunset, and for Jean and me, today would be no different. Our guide asked if we were sure we wanted to go, telling us to expect lots of flooded areas and much mud. "Of course we're sure we want to go," we told him. Our jeep slipped and slid for miles, finally coming to what had previously been a dry creek bed that was now full of water and mud. He thought we should get out until he was sure he could get safely across and make it up the boulders on the other side. No way! We held on tight and laughed uproariously with every slip and slide. All the guides agreed they had never had visitors who'd had as much fun or laughed as much as we did. We enjoy it all over again with every telling.

If you aren't laughing with us—or at us—you just don't understand!

COURAGE AND FAITH

"Would your son testify if we go to trial?" we were asked by the police. On trial would be the tough kid who had gouged another boy's eyes out during a gang fight, blinding him for life. That tough kid had tried to do the same to our son at an earlier wrestling match. After winning that match, Jeff was approached by the kid and asked to meet in the parking lot, which Jeff avoided. As parents, we wanted to say no. The kid was known to run with a rough crowd, and we worried about possible repercussions. Our son was sixteen, and we didn't want him at risk. Ultimately, though, it was his decision, and he testified. That same son had thrown the principal's son over his shoulder and taken him to the principal's office because he was bullying another boy. Risky! Thankfully, the principal understood that his son needed some correction. Our son understood that standing up for others required courage and conviction.

HERE COMES THE BRIDE

I was blessed with the perfect mother-in-law. When she took me under her wing, I had no clue how to be a daughter-in-law. I was young, far away from my family, and adjusting to being married to my "throw-the-rule-book-out-the-window" husband. When I was about to become a mother-in-law for the first time, I thought, *Oh gosh, I'm not like Mom. I'm not calm and sweet and gracious. How am I going to be a good mother-in-law?* My soon-to-be daughter-in-law made it easy.

She called one day and said, "Kathy, Mom and Bama and I are going to look at wedding dresses. Would you please come with us?" Stephanie's invitation to be part of such a special moment in her life with her mother and grandmother endeared her to me forever. It wasn't something that she had to do, and no one would have thought anything of it if she hadn't included me, but she did, and it meant the world to me. When I look back on sweet moments, Stephanie's invitation is one of the first ones that comes to mind.

CAN YOU SAY "TATTOO"?

You know by now that Kent was a rebel—a skipping-school, running-away-from-home kind of rebel—but one thing he has never been able to come to terms with is tattoos. He doesn't think anyone ought to have one. So, when our youngest, sweetest child, Jeff, went off to college and got a tattoo, nobody dared tell Kent about it.

I adjusted to the tattoo pretty quickly, but then Jeff pushed the envelope further. One day I went to see him at college, and when he came to the door, he was talking funny. I couldn't understand what he was saying, and then I saw it. I didn't say a word. I turned on my heels and walked around the building and cried. I thought for sure that tongue ring would condemn him to hell. Eventually, I adjusted to that too. Kent … not so much.

Shortly after Jeff got his first tattoo, the family was together for a pool party. Kent was still the only one in the dark, and Ray and Bryan were just hysterical watching Jeff in the pool playing with his nieces and nephews with his T-shirt on.

"Hey, Jeff," they taunted him. "Why don't you take your shirt off?"

I said, "Jeff, you're going to have to get over this. You knew Dad wouldn't like it, and you did it anyway, so you have to live with the consequences. Just take your shirt off."

Jeff took his shirt off and was still in the pool playing with the kids when Kent came out. We were all watching, trying not to laugh, and Jeff was doing his best to ignore Kent as he walked around the pool. After checking out all the goings on in the pool, Kent came to where we were all talking and laughing about the tattoo. Kent didn't say a word.

Ray turned to his brother and said, "Bryan, you might as well let Dad see yours too."

Kent scowled and said, "I want to see it."

Bryan said, "Dad, it's on my backside and I'm not showing you."

This went back and forth for a few minutes, and finally Kent told Ray, "You and Jeff are going to hold him down. I'm going to pull his shorts down, and I'm going to see it."

Bryan said, "Wait a minute, Dad. I have to go to the bathroom. When I come back, I'll show it to you." It was all very dramatic, and Bryan and his wife, Kerri, went into the house. Meanwhile, Kent still hadn't spoken a word to Jeff. When they came back out, Bryan said, "All right, Dad, since you insist." He pulled down his shorts, and on his right cheek in ink it said, "Gotcha."

That is one of our favorite funny family stories of all time. Kent still doesn't think it is as funny as the rest of us, but almost every Thanksgiving or Christmas, somebody tells this story, and we laugh just as hard as we did the first time.

I don't think Kent spoke to Jeff for a week, but then he got over it, because that's what families do. They disagree, argue, and sometimes need space from each other, but they are always there to support each other, to forgive each other, and to laugh together.

WE CAN DISAGREE, BUT FIRST WE ARE FAMILY

My brother, Gary, taught me that lesson. He and I could rarely agree on anything. If I said, "It's a beautiful day," he would reply with "Yeah, but it's going to get cold." And I would do the same to him. One day we were in some deep discussion that got heated—I don't even remember what we were arguing about that seemed so important at the time. I'm pretty verbal, and I was fiercely stating my case when he looked at me and said, "Okay, stop. Kathy, you are my sister; you are my family. We are going to agree to disagree on everything from here out with no discussion."

"Okay," I said, and that was that. After that we were able to have such good times together. As adults, I asked him about it.

He said, "I wasn't willing to win whether I was right or not, because I didn't want to fight with you. You're my family." And I really respected him for that and took it to heart. In his later years, I was aware of several significant decisions he made based on family loyalty. Family was always first for Gary.

My brother lost his brief fight with cancer in May of 2021. Jean and I were able to spend quite a bit of time with him in his last few months, for which I am grateful. He was a gentle but tough country boy. He never complained or begrudged that his life was coming to an end. I so respected the way he handled it and the way he lived his life.

Family first. Gary will always be my brother, and that is what Kent and I try to instill in our boys. You can be vastly different (and they are), you can disagree (and they do), but you will always be brothers, and there is nothing that can ever change that.

ENTERTAINMENT CHAIRMAN

One of the best gifts a partner or family can give you is balance. We all come with our own strengths and weaknesses, positive attributes along with a few negative ones here and there, and sometimes it takes someone else to help tip your scales to positive. Kent is my balance.

I've always been the serious, responsible one and a bit of a workaholic. If I wasn't working at the office, I'd be working at home. There were always things to be done, and what I thought of as Kent's lack of seriousness and shirking of responsibilities would infuriate me at times. I would often resist his encouragement to not take things too seriously and to relax and have some fun. Eventually, I learned to be grateful for his desire to entertain and keep me from working too hard or getting overwhelmed. Kent is the one who makes the entertainment plans and brings me along. If we go to the movies or dinner, Kent's the one who makes it happen. Even with activities that he is not going to participate in with me, Kent's the one who makes arrangements for me, always encouraging me to get out there and enjoy myself.

> **One of the best gifts a partner or family can give you is balance.**

Kent used to worry that if something ever happened to him, I'd just sit in my room and never do anything. While that may have been true a few years ago, it's definitely not the case now. In fact, the boys tell us that our roles have switched—I'm more laid back, and Kent is now the rule follower. Funny how that happens.

THINGS TO CONSIDER

- Make time to share special moments with individual family members.
- Teach your children to be brave and courageous.
- It's okay to disagree; protect relationships above all.
- To the best of your ability, assure all is well between family members.
- Appreciate the one who "takes you away from it all."
- Always stand up for others.

CHAPTER 9

GENERATIONS OF GENEROSITY

It is through the collection of memories and stories for this book that I have come to appreciate the legacy of generosity that generations of my family have provided me. They didn't talk about their generosity or preach it. They simply lived it, and I was fortunate to often be included in their acts of kindness (even if I didn't realize it at the time).

My father worked hard and made us work hard. He owned a small grocery, and I often helped him deliver groceries. I didn't think anything of it; it was just working with Dad. At my father's funeral, people came to me and said, "If it hadn't been for your dad, our family would have starved." Hearing those words from several people, I remembered all those times we delivered groceries. Not only was my dad giving away the groceries, but he was delivering them to the homes of these families so they wouldn't have to come into the store and be embarrassed when they couldn't pay for them. That's generosity and kindness at its best.

THE APPLE DOESN'T FALL FAR FROM THE TREE

My father's legacy of service to others was founded in his grandparents, my great-grandparents, Mama and Papa Savage. Their generation lived through two world wars, the Great Depression, and the Dust Bowl—terrible, tragic times. I never heard them complain about hardship or their own suffering. Papa was a tall, attractive man with silver hair and big blue eyes and the best laugh. He was always joyful despite, by most standards, his hard life. Instead, they exemplified what it means to be in service to others.

Papa was a constable, and his job was to go to communities that didn't have actual jails and collect prisoners. He'd travel to these communities by horse on Saturday and Sunday mornings after the drunken weekend brawls and bring the prisoners back to jail. On Sunday afternoon, after Mama fed them all a big home-cooked meal, Papa Savage would preach to them.

All of my dad's family were cut from the same cloth. My aunts and uncles, my father's siblings, are all generous and caring and concerned about others and always looking for ways to help people. The way they chose to live their lives had an impact on me. As a child, I wasn't cognizant of the extent of their kindness; I just loved them because they were family. When I tell my grandchildren these stories, they ask me why they did this or that, and that question "Why?" has given me pause to think about their actions differently and to fully appreciate the power of their graciousness.

WHEN YOU DON'T HAVE MUCH, YOU STILL HAVE ENOUGH TO GIVE

From my earliest memories of my mother's parents, who I called Mom and Pop Brown, both were retired. My sister and I sometimes wonder how they ever managed, because they sure didn't have much. But they did manage to survive, and my grandmother still found ways to give to others. I can remember so many times that my grandmother would sit down and write and donate to missionaries all over the world. She'd read the letters she received from those she supported and tell me all about them. Sometimes when she was getting her letters ready to send off, she'd say, "Kathy, you write a note and put it in there. Let them know you're praying for them and that you hope they're well." Many of the missionaries she supported were in Africa, and I often wonder if that early exposure is what made me fall in love with Africa and have such a strong desire to spend time there.

"It's time to go pick up the old folks for church." I can hear my grandmother's voice even now. Mom Brown was much older than anyone we ever picked up, but it was one of her many ways of helping others. She was faithful to them like she was faithful to the Lord. Mom Brown lived to be 101 years old. Toward the end of her life, she was bedridden and in a nursing home. She sometimes said to us, "I'm packed and ready to go home (meaning heaven). I'm not useful to the Lord anymore."

She had just said that to me during one of my last visits with her. As I was leaving, a woman approached me in the hall and asked if I was Mrs. Brown's granddaughter. She had just come from her elderly aunt's room and wanted to tell me thank you. I was puzzled. "Many people come to visit your grandmother, and she insists all of them stop by to see my aunt, who never has visitors otherwise." I turned back to Mom Brown's room to assure her she was still very useful to the Lord.

In a recent conversation with a cousin, we both agreed it was greatly in part to Mom Brown's faith that our own faith was made strong.

> *No matter what, no matter how hard a spot you're in, you've always got enough to give, to help somebody else.*
> —MOM BROWN

THE GIFT OF HOSPITALITY

While I can't claim Kent's mother as a blood relative, Mom Stone became my family the moment we met. Her kind and generous spirit impacted me greatly, and I am grateful for the legacy of generosity that she has bestowed upon Kent, our boys, and our grandchildren.

When Mom was just sixteen, a missionary visited their church in Helena, Montana, and talked about the severe conditions in an orphanage in Egypt. He told the congregation that if one of the baby girls got sick, they would put them in a room and leave them to die. It was only the boys whom they tried to save.

Mom was so touched by the story she decided to go to Egypt. The story is that she took a train from Helena to New York and from there boarded a ship to England. From England, she boarded another ship that brought her to Egypt. She made her way to Egypt all by herself. The plan was for her to do missionary work there for one year. Mom stayed three years because the need was so great. I don't think many sixteen-year-olds or even adults would make that choice.

I am honored to have seen her generosity in action. Mom didn't have a lot of money to give; her gift was hospitality. She prepared meals for weddings or the celebration of a new baby or because someone was sick or homebound. She served as a volunteer ambassador for the state of Hawaii for visiting dignitaries. She would tour them around the island and then welcome them into her home for a family dinner. She would set the table with beautiful and unusual pieces of china that had been handed down by her family over the years. I would ask her, "Aren't you worried that they'll get broken?"

"Here's a lesson," she said. "It's not worth anything if you hide it. Whatever you have, you share it."

That's a lesson I still carry with me today. I remember one Christmas several years after Mom Stone had gone to be with the Lord, as I prepared dinner and the table for my children and grandchildren, I carefully chose the Christmas dishes and glassware we would use. At the back of a bureau drawer were three carefully wrapped items. Opening them, I admired my mother-in-law's silver.

Just spoons, forks, and knives—only six of each, not enough for even half of those coming to dinner. I began rewrapping them in their soft and safe coverings to replace them in the back of the drawer. Suddenly tears sprang unbidden, along with a wish she was here to lay the silver out and see our beautiful family.

"Mom" or "Tutu," the affectionate Hawaiian term for grandmother, came to memory in real life, and I realized how much I missed her. It's just eighteen pieces of silver ... no, it's years of love, advice, example, fun, acceptance ... and her youngest son, my husband of fifty-three years. How I wish she were at our table this Christmas. I'm grateful for her spoons, forks, and knives and for sweet memories of a wonderful woman.

CONTINUING THE LEGACY OF GENEROSITY

I was at a women's conference about twenty-five years ago. A representative from Christian-based nonprofit World Vision passed around envelopes with pictures of children and asked for people to sponsor a child. Envelopes kept coming, and I kept passing them along until the picture of this little boy made me stop and hold it tight. I couldn't pass along the envelope that belonged to Noel Jackson, and I thought, *Surely we can manage twenty-nine dollars per month to help this child.* I immediately signed us up, and that was our first connection to World Vision.

A few years later, a young woman, Deborah, a philanthropic recruiter for World Vision, moved to Dallas when her husband was transferred to the area. One day she called and asked me if I ever thought about getting more involved with World Vision and would I consider hosting donors in my home. I had never thought about it before, but Deborah was the sweetest woman in the world, and there was no way I could say no to her. I called her my gentle nudger. She was the motivation I needed to get more involved and learn more about the organization, and Kent and I have been committed to the mission of World Vision ever since.

We have sponsored numerous children over the years and have been to Honduras twice to meet families the organization supports. We visited one community in Honduras where the only water available was from a muddy, green, stagnant stream that the cattle drank out of and defecated in. The children walked two hours every morning to fetch water for the day. Disease is prevalent because of the contaminated water they are forced to rely on. World Vision helped coordinate the development of a well. There was a water source at the top of a nearby mountain, and the man who owned it donated the land to the community. The members of the community went to work digging a five-mile trench down the mountain.

We had the honor of being there the day they turned the water on. The joy, hope, and gratitude the people had for the gift of clean water was beyond anything I had experienced. We were humbled to witness such gratitude and joy for something many of us take for granted every single day of our lives. This community now has a stable source of clean water. Helping communities become self-sustaining is a primary goal of World Vision.

We've been involved with the organization for over twenty-five years and have passed along the importance of philanthropy to our boys. Ray, Bryan, and Jeff are all supportive of World Vision, but they also have their own charitable pursuits. Jeff's family is involved in Seed Effect in Uganda. Bryan's family participates in mission trips every year in South Texas, where there is extreme poverty right here in our home state. Ray and Steph founded their own Instagram account @finderofmoney. Ray teaches teens that you can take "found money," accumulate and invest it, have patience, and in future years reap enough to do well, with the ultimate goal of becoming a millionaire and giving it away.

The idea of @finderofmoney resulted from long walks during which they would find coins on the street or in parking lots. Maybe they'd find twenty-five cents one morning and more the next. It sounds small and silly, but it got Ray thinking how everyone says they can't build a financial base, much less give away money, after paying all their bills. This also led them to found a family charity where even the youngest grandchild has a part and a vote on which charity benefits each year.

Check out www.WorldVisionInternational.org to learn more about humanitarian efforts around the world.

Generosity isn't just about money. Be generous with love, time, sharing your talents and skills. Everyone has something to give. Do so generously!

We've all had times when we've struggled. When Kent and I were young and struggling and living in an hourly motel and couldn't buy a house, I had many moments of despair. Looking back, I remember so much of my time spent worrying and crying and just not being able to see a way out. But then I realized that I could be grateful for what was good—our two wonderful children, my husband who was working hard to build a business that would improve our lives—and my gratitude became bigger than my despair.

Years later, during another challenging time in my life, someone gave me a gratitude journal. Every day I had to write down something that I was grateful for, and it reminded me that the good in my life far outweighed the challenges. When you are grateful, when you truly see all that you do have, your heart opens to the service of others. My father, Kent's parents, and our grandparents always saw what they had rather than what they didn't, and their hearts were filled with generosity.

THINGS TO CONSIDER

- Be kind and generous always.
- Seek out and help those in need.
- Small amounts multiply with faith.
- Generosity isn't just about money. Think of ways you can practice it.
- Don't hide things—share them!
- Teach generosity to everyone you influence.

CHAPTER 10

THE POWER OF ONE

We all make choices, and we are responsible for the consequences of those choices. We can choose to give, to receive, to take. We can choose to be kind or unforgiving, responsible or irresponsible. No matter what choices we make, those choices will impact others. The words we choose to speak, the actions we choose to take, the example we choose to set can inspire or dishearten those around us. I encourage you to appreciate the power of your influence on others and to choose wisely how you wield it. I am grateful for those individuals who have chosen to use their influence to inspire and encourage me.

A STANDARD OF EXCELLENCE

Most of us recall a teacher who made us believe in ourselves and encouraged us to stretch ourselves further than we thought we could go. For me, that was my high school business teacher, Mr. Farmer. I can't say he was a gentle teacher; in fact, he was very demanding. But he was a gentle person who demanded excellence from his students.

We had competitions in typing and shorthand, and I was a state champion because Mr. Farmer instilled in me that it wasn't about being the fastest. It was always, always about being your personal best. He taught us not to just get by but to push for excellence. The reason for competition, he told us, was not to beat or downgrade someone else but to continually improve yourself, and, if you did your best, to not feel bad if you didn't win.

He was an amazing teacher who taught long after I graduated. At his funeral a few years ago, there were current students, former students who were parents, grandparents, and every age in between. His influence reached many people over several generations.

I'M NOT AFRAID (ANYMORE)

My mother was a paradox. She was feisty. She was harsh. She was also loving. The life lessons she taught me didn't always seem at the time as if they were born out of love, but as an adult and a parent myself, I now understand that she was teaching me to stand on my own and face my fears.

When I was about ten years old, we lived out in the country, and behind our house was a big hedge. Beyond the hedge was the gate that kept the cattle fenced in. After dinner, the table scraps had to be taken out to the dogs. There were no lights, and it was a long walk, especially in the dark with the sounds of the wild animals lurking on the edges. It was my job to take the scraps out. I would try to convince my brother to do it. I would beg my dad to do it. But they flat-out refused. My mom would always say, "Kathy, remember to walk; don't run." One night I remember more vividly than others. I was more spooked than usual, but I made sure to walk out there.

I finally reached the dogs, emptied the scraps into their dishes, and turned and sprinted for the house.

Mom was standing on the porch, and when I reached her, she said, "Okay, now turn around, walk out there, and stand for a while until I call you. Then *walk* back." She could see how scared I was, but she still made me do it. What I wanted was for her to hug me and tell me everything was going to be all right, but that wasn't going to happen. I walked back out as I was told, stood waiting for her to call me, and then walked back to the house as slowly as I could, desperately fighting the urge to run.

My mother could have told me everything was all right, but instead she taught me to realize it for myself. Looking back, I now understand there were a lot of lessons she taught me that didn't feel like lessons at the time. Learning to face my fears opened my world to opportunities I may not have taken otherwise. Hot-air ballooning, skydiving, parasailing, riding a Harley, traveling in foreign countries alone. Would I have eagerly done all those things if not for her lessons?

JUST SHOW UP

Pop Brown never wore anything but khaki pants, a starched khaki shirt, and an old felt brown hat. He smoked a pipe, he ate oatmeal, and I bet I never heard him say ten words my whole life—and he never, ever left the house. When I told my grandmother that I was getting married, she said, "Now don't get your feelings hurt, but you know Pop won't come to your wedding. You know he loves you, but he's not going to come." I told her that I knew that and that I understood.

When I walked into the church on my wedding day, Pop was the first person I saw. He was sitting in the back row, and as my dad and I passed, I stopped, leaned over, and gave him a big hug and a kiss.

He didn't say a word or show any emotion, but I knew what it meant for him to show up for me like that.

AND KEEP SHOWING UP

I was a member of Bible Study Fellowship, and my first year there, our teaching leader's mother passed away. I think I had hardly even spoken to her personally at the time, but I felt compelled to attend her mother's funeral. I stayed in the back and never approached her.

The following year, she reached out and asked me to become a group leader. I was surprised and asked, "How do you even know who I am?" (Our class had around five hundred members.) "You came to my mother's funeral. You didn't even know me and didn't know my mother at all, but you showed up, and that meant a lot."

Several of my friends did the same for me when my dad died. My dad was buried in a tiny out-of-the-way town in South Texas, six hours from where my friends lived. When I walked into the church, eight friends who I had never expected to come were there. They didn't ask. They didn't make a big deal out of it. They just showed up. Sometimes people don't put themselves into difficult situations because they don't know what to say. You don't have to know what to do or what to say; simply showing up makes all the difference in the world.

TAKING A CHANCE

In 1982, our business was still in a stage that required us to put all our money back into the business. As a result, we had sold our home a couple of years before and were renting a house that was much too small for our growing family. We were eager to be homeowners again. We figured we could manage a $250,000 mortgage, but we needed to find a house that didn't require any money down. I didn't think it was possible, and I said to Kent, "We've been through some tough times, and we've been able to dig ourselves out, but there is a limit to this pie-in-the-sky thinking." But there was no limit for Kent. One Sunday after church, we set out to look for houses that wouldn't require a down payment. After a few hours, we were overwhelmed and decided to cut the search short and escape to an afternoon at the movies.

While standing in line, we looked back to see a couple we knew from our Sunday school class. We stepped out of line to join them. They asked what we were doing, and we told them we were out looking for a house but that we got discouraged and came to the movies instead. He asked what kind of house we were looking for, and we told him, "In the $250,000 range, but we don't have even a penny to put toward a down payment."

He looked at us and said, "I have one of those."

"Yeah, right," we both said with a laugh.

"No, really, I do. In fact, I have two houses."

We didn't know Don was a builder. It was spring of 1980 when he and his partner had built these two homes just prior to the recession that hit that January. As a result, they hadn't been able to sell them. He offered to show them to us.

I said, "We really would love to be able to buy a house with nothing down, but we aren't seriously thinking about it right now."

"Just come take a look," he said, "and see what you think."

We looked, and of course fell in love with one of them. He said he would talk to his partner and see what they could come up with.

We bought the house for $250,000 with no money down and moved in within a month. The builders carried a three-year note on what would have been the down payment. We made the mortgage payment, paid them a monthly note, and ended up paying it off early.

They didn't charge us any interest for those three years. When they sold the second house, they did the same thing for those new owners. Their willingness to take a chance on us significantly impacted our lives. That house became our home for the next twenty-one years.

PAYING IT FORWARD

Kent and I have benefited from the positive influence of so many, and it is our hope that we have done and will continue to do the same for others. That was one of the big draws for us with the directorship: it provided us the opportunity to be personally impactful—to be the power of one for others. Two specific experiences come to mind: the partnership franchise between Jeff and Wilbur, and solo franchise owner Natalie.

When we first met Jeff, Wilbur, and their wonderful families, they were generating about $450,000 a year, a median income for a franchise in our industry at that time. They'd owned the franchise for five years but weren't really growing. When Kent was visiting with them one day, he just asked, "Why are you still doing that same volume? What's holding you back?"

"Well, isn't that about all we can do in a small area like we are in?" they asked.

"No," said Kent. "You can do anything you want to."

Within three years, Jeff and Wilbur were generating several million dollars a year. In 2021, they generated over $18 million. More importantly, they believed in themselves and are now living their dreams, which includes charitable work. I cannot imagine the lives they have been able to impact with that resource and their generosity. One of their current missions is being mentors to other franchises. One of those is our grandson's. Still today, more than ten years later, I receive devotionals from Jeff every day, and quite often he'll say, "Just a reminder that you and your family had a huge impact on our lives. We are so grateful."

Sometimes, you just need someone to believe in you so you can believe in yourself. Paying it forward brings it full circle.

The same was true for Natalie. Natalie and her husband had been running a successful franchise when personal issues tore their family apart and nearly ran their business into the ground. By the time they divorced, the franchise was generating only $105,000, which was not enough to support her family. Natalie was determined not only to survive but to make sure she would be independent, not relying on anyone to provide for her family.

One day she came to us and said, "I have to make this work. I have to learn how to run this business." Her *why* was bigger than her fear of failure. Natalie worked hard and focused on succeeding, overcoming all kinds of difficulties. She turned her business around, and it's still successful today. Several years ago, she met and married a delightful young man, and they run the business together. Kent and I are honored to have been able to offer Natalie encouragement and support along her path to success—success that resulted from her smart choices and hard work.

> **Sometimes, you just need someone to believe in you so you can believe in yourself. Paying it forward brings it full circle.**

I believe we all need to acknowledge those who have influenced and impacted our life in a positive way and find ways to be that person who positively influences and impacts others. Challenge yourself every day to ask yourself, "Who in my life do I need to thank? Whom do I have the opportunity to influence? Whose life might be better?"

THINGS TO CONSIDER

- Recognize and appreciate those who have influenced and impacted your life and family.
- Remember lessons parents and others instilled in you that you may not have acknowledged.
- Showing up is the most important thing you can do.
- Take chances on people; help them believe in themselves.
- Pay it forward. Exercise your power of one.

PART IV

COLLECTED ESSAYS

ALWAYS FLYING IN MY DREAMS

When I was a little girl, my nighttime dreams almost always included flying. I'd be standing in an open field, eyes closed, concentrating really hard, and slowly I'd rise over the trees, floating above the earth. It was an awesome feeling. Inevitably, I'd lose focus and down I'd come. The dream would come another night, and once again I would be soaring.

I hadn't thought about those dreams until, as an adult, I went parasailing in Mexico. The sensation of being lifted and then floating was familiar and wonderful. Since that first time, I've parasailed, flown in a glider plane, rode a ParaPlane, and floated in a hot-air balloon more than once. Then there were the rolls and loops and landing "elevator" style, all while strapped into the open cockpit of a Mustang trainer.

All were fun and exciting.

But by far the best experience was the day we were riding Harleys and ended up at a skydiving field. Unknown to me, several of our riders had reservations to go up that day. I wished I had known!

As we arrived, people were frantically running around screaming, "Runaway, runaway!" Someone's parachute hadn't opened, and there was momentary panic until the emergency chute finally ballooned out. Terrifying to say the least, but not a reason for the riders in our group to chicken out. The first one was a young teen. When she and the instructor landed, it was evident something was not right. They were quickly sprayed down with a water hose. The teen had eaten two cheeseburgers just before making her flight. Very messy!

By now, some of the riders were having second thoughts. Bonnie bravely hoisted her parachute and got on the small Cessna. "Whatever you do, don't plant your feet upon reaching the ground—bend your knees and run," the instructor said. She forgot, planted her feet firmly upon landing, and before the ambulance arrived, her broken ankle swelled to the size of her thigh. Ouch!

Several others decided it might not be the day for parachuting and backed out. As the ambulance pulled out with Bonnie and her swollen ankle, the leader hollered out that there was an open space. "Would anyone like to go up?"

I shot my hand up. "I'll go."

Perception is a funny thing. I have never considered myself a risk taker and really still don't today. But here I was, raising my hand to skydive after witnessing three failed attempts, and beside me Kent, my risk-taking husband, was yelling, "What, are you crazy?" Kent had no desire to strap on a parachute and jump out of a plane. He was not thrilled that I was going to do it.

The instructor put a piece of paper in front of me that basically said, "You're getting on a run-down plane with a pilot who doesn't know what he's doing. Sign here." I was so excited that I didn't think twice. When they opened the door at ten thousand feet, I admit I was scared, and I said bad words that a good Christian girl like me isn't supposed to say. But I loved it. As I stood gaping out at thin air, the instructor told me to step out onto the *tiny* step (it had looked much bigger on the ground) and reach for the strut. We would jump on the count of three. I don't know what happened to the count of three, but the moment I touched the strut, I was falling into that nothingness.

Free-falling was the most exciting, exhilarating, and flat-out fun thing I have ever done. It's fast and hard to catch your breath. I couldn't stop laughing. There was only one problem: it was over entirely too fast. Once the chute opens, it's a slow, quiet drift, and you have a minute to take in the view, including the very small area in which you are supposed to land. It's nice, but not the rush of that free fall.

It was the most exciting thing I've ever done, and I would do it again, except my risk-taking husband has asked me not to.

So, what's my fascination with flying, and how does my not being a risk taker fit into this? It's the rush, the freedom you feel, and the perspective you have from the air. It's the thrill and excitement that is way bigger than any fear. Or maybe it's that childhood dream coming to life. Some who know me wonder about my stability and what on earth could possess me to make me do these crazy, spontaneous things. I see myself as conservative in values, money, and what I perceive as right. I guess it just doesn't extend to fun and challenging things like marrying in a week, moving repeatedly, or going into business ... or flying adventures.

TO MY GRANDDAUGHTERS

The wonderful, amazing woman I am going to tell you about was many things.

This woman could be hilarious. Yet I never heard her express humor at the expense of someone else; never was she cruel, unkind, disrespectful, or belittling.

She lived in an "old white man's world"—her grandfather, father, husband, employers, customers. Yet I never once heard her bemoan the difficulty of her life because of being a woman.

She was smart, self-educated, well spoken, outspoken, feisty, traveled, and highly respected by all who knew her. "Old white men" sought her counsel throughout her adult life.

She was born at a time when women stayed home, kept quiet, and didn't make trouble. She didn't stay home, didn't keep quiet (about important things), and wasn't afraid of a little trouble if it was for a good reason.

She worked until she was eighty-five, drove her own car until well into her nineties, was a church and community leader, owned her own home, was debt-free, and was loved by all. She had friends around the world due mostly to her support of foreign missionaries and other worthwhile causes. She supported both herself and her husband for many years and never asked for or received financial help from anyone or from the government. She traveled to Cuba in the fifties—a time when women did not travel to such places and certainly didn't travel alone.

She picked up "old people" for church, community activities, and grocery shopping. I never saw one of them who wasn't younger than her. Her life was one of kindness and service. She lived through two world wars and the Korean and Vietnam wars; through the Great Depression, the civil rights movement, and segregation; through recessions, droughts, wayward children, and the illness and death of loved ones. I never heard her complain about any of it.

She was never on television or the national news, never performed on stage or wrote a book. She did, however, influence thousands of lives in and far beyond her small-town environment. She respected people and was respected.

She was funny, full of grace, loved the Lord and her family, and was a servant to many. She was a strong woman of character.

My prayer is that when you are looking for someone to follow, to be like, you will think of her. I was privileged to know her personally and wish you could have. She would have so loved each of you.

Her name was Blanche Rossie Slater Brown. She was your great-great-grandmother.

SCHOOL SUPPLIES, BEETS, AND GREEN TORTILLAS

What could these things possibly have in common? Or people from Colorado, Texas, and Honduras? We have a great and mighty God who weaves a thread through time, people, places, and events to accomplish good for His people.

A small group of individuals from various locations, ages seventeen to seventy-six and with very different backgrounds, came together to be God's hands and feet for His purpose. Everything in the above title became a part of this story.

"Want to go back to Honduras?" Or maybe, "Want to go to Honduras for the first time?" Nine of us said yes, and we were off! On a previous trip, some of us had visited a school that had virtually no resources. Three godly women in our group purchased boxes and boxes of school supplies! We all were blessed to be a part of it by sorting, packing, and distributing them.

You should have seen the teachers' eyes!

This was part of THRIVE, World Vision's program to improve economic development through farming. From struggling small family plots to a beautiful community garden with corn, beans, tomatoes, peppers, and a new experiment—beets! Sixteen thousand tiny beet plants just waiting to go into the carefully prepared ground. So, plant we did. No, not all; just one row.

You should have seen their pride. Not only in their beets and other thriving crops but in the area they had set aside to train another community how to do the same.

Improving nutrition, especially for children, is another part of World Vision's program to improve the lives of the most vulnerable of God's children. Now off to a nutritional center at a kindergarten to see how it works in the field. Children who previously may have been lethargic or even ill from malnutrition are now happy, well, active, and attending school regularly. They welcomed us with smiles and clapping and sat quietly while their teacher spoke to us about the hardships and progress.

Then to the kitchen where we served the children soy milk and chopped fresh greens and stirred a beautiful concoction of tomatoes and green peppers. The greens were added to a soy mixture, and we laughingly tried to form small tortillas for the experts (moms). They were quickly fried, and a nutritious lunch was ready.

You should have seen those happy, smiling faces of children now healthier because of good nutrition.

You should have seen the humble gratitude of the people. You should have seen their tears for the future of their children.

You should have seen their love for and trust in God.

You should have seen their hardships and their resilience. You should have seen their love for the amazing people of World Vision who give selflessly with clear devotion to make a difference in Honduras.

You should have seen our tears and sensed our broken hearts.

You should have seen the joy and hope of the people of Honduras.

SOLOMON'S WISDOM

One evening when our granddaughters Olivia (age eight) and Charlotte (age six) were staying with Kent and me, I realized the noise level was rising more than I thought acceptable, so I called the girls to me. Olivia was upset because Charlotte wanted a blue pencil back that she had originally given to Olivia. Nothing I said solved the problem, and both ended up in tears. So, I told them the story of King Solomon, about his wisdom from God, and about the two women who both wanted the one baby. Both were horrified when I said King Solomon suggested giving half the baby to each woman as a solution, since neither was willing to give up the baby. Of course, I was holding the blue pencil up in front of them the whole time.

After giving them a second to consider Solomon's solution, I asked if they would be okay with me breaking the blue pencil in half and giving each of them a piece. "*No!*" both said. When I asked what they thought the women did, they figured it all out. Olivia willingly gave up the pencil, at which time Charlotte said, "No, Olivia can have the pencil. I'll take the eraser." They ran off laughing (at me, I suppose), happy and sharing. Solomon's wisdom is still working today. I thank God for that.

TO MY GRANDSONS

T-shirts and baseball caps from the Holy Land just didn't seem appropriate, besides the fact that you all have more than enough of those. As I thought about what I could bring you to let you know I thought of you while there, I sent a prayer to God thanking him for each of you and asking his protection over you.

While each of you have very special and individual traits, you do have at least one thing in common: your last name. Stone, or Pohaku in Hawaiian. This name is a bond that can never be broken, and it ties you to generations of amazing people you will never know this side of heaven.

It is a bond I want you to always be fully aware of as brothers and as cousins. Growing up, I was quite a bit older than most of my cousins, but I was recently reminded of the strength and depth of family relations as one of them said to me at a funeral for a favored uncle, "Kathy, if you ever need anything, you know you can call me or any of us, right?"

Stone has a pretty obvious meaning to most: rock. If you look a bit further, it also means strength of character, foundation, truth, steadfastness, resoluteness, great strength, power, and preciousness (as gems). My favorite of these is strength of character, because I see that in each of you.

The bracelet you are holding was handcrafted at the Dead Sea in Israel. The word on it is Hebrew for Stone. I chose Stone instead of first names to remind you of this thing that ties you together. Each of you has exactly the same bracelet. Perhaps you will wear it, perhaps not. Perhaps one day you will pass it on to your son or grandson. Or maybe to a daughter or granddaughter?

I love you deeply.

WALK 714 MILES IN MY SHOES

Third grade, sunny spring afternoon, girls' PE, baseball. The batter was tall and athletic and hit the ball, which I realized with terror was heading straight toward me. I was a quick-minded eight-year-old and immediately knew I had to run for it. And I did. Right off the field. No sweating, no physical harm, and no embarrassment at not catching the ball. Safe! Once again confirming my belief that I was simply not created for physical activity.

Grading papers and volunteering for anything the teacher needed pretty much kept me out of PE and any form of physical activity for the rest of my school years. Well, there was the two-year stint as a cheerleader, but as I managed to be "head" cheerleader, we sure didn't do splits, chorus line kicks, and such during my reign.

There were other signs of my inept physical self, such as crying throughout swim lessons when I was ten and driving from Dillard's to Macy's in the shopping mall as an adult. Oh, I did the occasional exercise program, but not for long, and I didn't sweat.

Fast-forward to October 2011 and a decision that losing thirty-five pounds was necessary and would certainly require more than never eating again. I would start walking regularly. Yay for me! I started in January, and by early summer, my son challenged me to do a 5K in our neighborhood.

"Most people will walk, Mom," my son assured me. When I asked my son what my goal should be, he said, "To finish." Needing a bit more clarity than that, I asked him how long it should take me "to finish." He did a bit of research and advised that women my age doing 5Ks in the area were finishing in forty-seven minutes. That was the slowest time.

My goal was to finish in forty-five minutes.

Race day came. It was an eighty-five-degree day in Dallas, Texas, in July. Thirty friendly neighbors were lined up at the starting line. At exactly 9:00 a.m., the starting gun fired ... and off they all went—running! My son had lied to me!

Clearly I was not going to make my target time of forty-five minutes by walking. Being a naturally prideful person, I did not want to come in last. My son and Kent paced me throughout and let me know several times I had to step it up in order to finish within my set time goal. I sweated, panted, walked briskly, and, of course, had to run part of the time (my body was shocked!). I did it, and I didn't come in last. My husband and son sweetly came in after me.

The news of my mighty accomplishment must have gotten out, because not long after that, during a friendly conversation among girlfriends, someone suggested I consider doing the Susan G. Komen 3-Day for the Cure for breast cancer. I don't actually recall saying okay, but one way or another I got on the "walking list." Training was long and serious; walking became my life. First, summer heat and sweating (I discovered my body could do that without melting), choosing shoes, planning routes, forgoing other activities like movies and dinner, moving to early cold mornings with fleece pants, gloves, headgear (ruins the hairdo). During training we walked over 650 miles. Survival became cause for celebration. On November 1, 2013, four of us joined twelve hundred other walkers and began the three-day journey of twenty miles each day and sleeping in tiny pink tents each night. Day 1: not too bad. Day 2: fell into the tent in tears. Day 3: okay, not so bad; we can do this. Done!

Here is a list of my lessons learned:

- God gave me an amazing body that is capable of so much more than I ever asked of it.
- There are bigger reasons to do something than personal accomplishment.
- Training and preparation are vital.
- Challenges are exhilarating.
- I need someone to expect more of me.
- The support and encouragement of family and friends helped more than I expected.
- The bigger purpose/goal made it possible to sacrifice time and other activities.
- Our strong team leader was important at every phase and moment (thank you, Cindy!).
- The goal was bigger and more important than my past, my age, my time, or my fears.
- Personal benefits were secondary but huge: weight loss, health, feeling of personal accomplishment, fun with friends, confi-

dence, appreciation for amazing support, beautiful sunrises, fresh air, and so much more.

- Now that it's over, it's much harder to maintain the walking, because that *big* goal isn't before me. The challenge is gone, the focus and commitment gone.

- I need a new and bigger goal and to apply all these lessons to the rest of my goals and my life!

CONCLUSION

My sister recently gave me two wall hangings. One says, "Start each day with God, grace, and gratitude." Good advice, don't you think? The other says, "Some days I amaze myself. Others I put laundry in the oven." That may just summarize my life. There have been many lessons—some easy; some not so much. I've learned from both the good and the bad and from the many people who have moved through my life.

There are many stories, and perhaps one day someone in my family will pick up their pen and continue our legacy. Their stories will be different but will continue the thread we have begun, tying us to our past and providing a bridge for future generations. I hope my stories have entertained you, encouraged you, and piqued your curiosity to think differently about some things. My sincerest hope, though, is that you will find time and energy to write your own stories. You have a story to tell, a legacy to share. I hope you will do that!

There you have it!

And we know that God causes all things to work together for good to those who love God, to those who are called according to His purpose.
—ROMANS 8:28

For the Lord is good. His lovingkindness is everlasting and His faithfulness to all generations.
—PSALM 100:5

ABOUT THE AUTHOR

Kathy Stone—philanthropist, entrepreneur, business leader, wife, friend, and mother—has built her life on a foundation of deep Christian values and a personal sense of purpose to always do her best and to help others. Along the way, she learned that being "right" isn't always what's most important, that the world won't end if you don't always follow "the rules," and that sometimes life is just supposed to be fun.

Kathy loves travel, music, art, and reading, but most important is her family—all who live nearby and who bring her unimaginable joy.

www.ingramcontent.com/pod-product-compliance
Lightning Source LLC
LaVergne TN
LVHW090116080426
835507LV00040B/939